Walking on the
MENDIP HILLS
TWELVE CIRCULAR WALKS OF DISCOVERY

Sue Gearing

HALSGROVE

First published in Great Britain by Halsgrove, 1999

ISBN 184114 023 6

Cataloguing in Publication Data

A CIP record for this title is available from the British Library

HALSGROVE
Publishing, Media & Distribution
Halsgrove House,
Lower Moor Way,
Tiverton, Devon
EX16 6SS

Telephone: 01884 243242
Facsimile: 01884 243325
e-mail: sales@halsgrove.com

Printed in Great Britain by
The Devonshire Press, Torquay

CONTENTS

Dedication 5

Acknowledgements 6

Walking Safely and Enjoyably 7

Introduction 9

The Walks (all circular)
It is difficult accurately to time walks; as a guideline allow a good hour for every 2 miles so that you have time to take in all that you see.

1. Western Bracer
Christon – Shiplate Slait – Bleadon – Hutton Hill – Upper Canada – Christon: 7.5 miles 11

2. A Line into the Past
Axbridge – Winscombe – Sandford Hill – Shipham – Winterhead – Fry's Hill – Axbridge: 8 miles (shorter alternative: 6 miles) 18

3. Dramatic Dolebury
Burrington Combe – Mendip Lodge – Dolebury – Rowberrow – Black Down – Burrington.Combe: 6.4 miles 28

4. Discovering Burrington
Burrington Ham – Burrington Camp – Rickford – Blagdon – Burrington Ham: 5.5 miles (shorter alternative: 4.5 miles) 36

5. The Heart of Mendip
Charterhouse – Blackmoor Reserve – Beacon Batch – Longwood Nature Reserve – Velvet Bottom – Charter-house: 5.75 miles (shorter alternative: 4.5 miles) 46

6. In and Around the Gorge
Wells – Underwood Quarry – Ebbor Nature Reserve and Gorge – Wookey Hole – Arthur's Point – Wells: 5.2 miles 55

7. Harptree Country
Harptree Hill – Smitham Chimney – East Harptree – Harptree Combe – Harptree Hill: 5.5 miles 63

8. Beauty on the Northern Edge
Hinton Blewett – Litton – Cameley – Hinton Blewett: 6.5 miles (shorter walk: 5.4 miles)   **71**

9. Green and Undulating
Dinder – Worminster – Croscombe – Dinder: 6.4 miles   **80**

10. Past the Lost Village
Nettlebridge – Ashwick Grove – Stoke Bottom – Edford Meadows – Harridge Wood – Nettlebridge: 5.5 miles (shorter alternative: 3.25 miles)   **87**

11. In the Footsteps of the Miners
Coleford – Vobster Coke Ovens – Vobster – Coleford: 5.3 miles   **94**

12. Beauty Masks an Industrial Past
Mells – Conduit Bridge – Barrow Hill – Buckland Dinham – Great Elm – Mells Stream – Mells: 6 miles   **103**

Reference Material   **112**

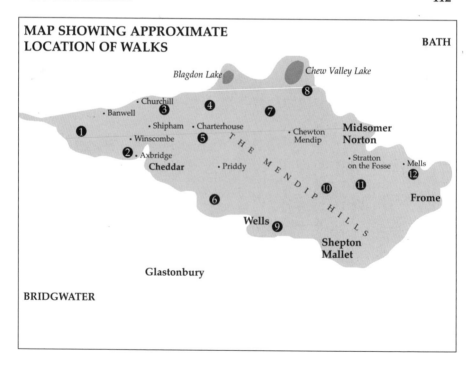

MAP SHOWING APPROXIMATE LOCATION OF WALKS

I couldn't have completed all the footwork for this book without my walking companions: my husband Peter, my friends Pat and Jane, and Jessie, my black labrador friend. This book is dedicated to them. A very special thank you goes to Jessie for her enthusiasm in coming out with me in all weathers and for covering more Mendip miles than any of us.

ACKNOWLEDGEMENTS

A great many local people, farmers, wildlife and local history experts have helped with putting me on the right track in the Mendips. I should particularly like to thank Pat Walter of the Mendip Society for her inspirations, research and footwork; Les Davies of the Mendip Warden Service for his unfailing enthusiasm and advice, and the Mendip rangers Dave Parker and Mike Chipperfield for painstakingly walking the routes; Chris Richards of the North Somerset Museum Service for his historical and geological knowledge; the Somerset Wildlife Trust; Bristol Water; Penny Stokes of Mendip District Council; Rights of Way Officers Sheila Petherbridge, Jim Docherty and Colin Hudson.

Thanks are also due to Wookey Hole Caves and Butcombe Brewery for their financial contribution to the publication of this book.

WALKING SAFELY AND ENJOYABLY

The aim of this book is to encourage responsible access to the Mendip Hills when walking. As a general rule, remember that, while the Mendip Hills are both beautiful and interesting, they can also be frightening and hostile if you are lost, cold or tired. The walks in this book are intended to be simple, straightforward and enjoyable, but they are not 'strolls in the park'. Every attempt has been made to ensure that they follow proper routes, but the Mendips are a living and changing environment. The seasons, weather and conditions on the ground all bring changes to the natural world and walkers must be realistic about their fitness, exercise commonsense and be responsible for their own well-being.

The Mendip Hills Warden Service has helped compile the following tips for walkers:

• Wear stout shoes with good grips or boots for walking and take a waterproof. Have enough clothing to keep warm when the sun goes in: the wind chill factor can be extreme on Mendip in winter. Several layers of clothing are better than one thick jumper. Particularly in summer when walking through bracken and undergrowth, cover legs and arms, and wear socks to avoid picking up ticks, which can carry Lyme disease; check your skin and your dog's coat for ticks. (A leaflet on Lyme disease is available from the Mendip Warden Service at Charterhouse).

• The sketch maps in this book are designed to keep you on the right track. It is recommended to have an Ordnance Survey Map as well. If you do lose your way, head downhill – nowhere on Mendip is more than a couple of miles from a road or farmhouse.

• Walk with care along narrow lanes, remembering that farm vehicles, as well as local and holiday traffic, use even the smallest road.

• Take care not to disturb grazing animals and keep dogs under strict control. They can disturb deer, which lie up in woodland and undergrowth, and are a particular danger to sheep during the lambing season. Despite its name, common land is private and walkers have no automatic right of access except on public footpaths.

• Camping and lighting fires are not allowed without the landowner's permission. Please take all litter home with you.

- Respect property. Do not climb over the drystone walls or dislodge stones from them. Use gates and stiles and remember to shut gates behind you. Leave water troughs, ponds, pools and streams undisturbed.

- Don't pick wild flowers; leave them for others to enjoy. Avoid making the kind of noise which will disturb birds and animals. Adders are more frightened of you than you are of them; adder bites are rare, but it's advisable to treat these snakes with respect.

- If you can, walk with someone or in a group. This applies especially in winter. Let someone know where you are going and what time you expect to be home. If you do get lost or need help, keep calm and remember that help is unlikely to be more than half an hour's walk away.

- Resist the temptation of exploring the caves or ruined buildings that you encounter. Both are dangerous.

- Park sensibly. Use car parks where possible and do not block gateways or narrow roads. There are very few tracks on which you can drive a vehicle or ride a motor cycle.

- If you find a blocked footpath, dangerous stile, or other hazard or obstruction, telephone the Mendip Hills Warden's Service on 01761 462338. Regular information from walkers is helpful to the wardens. Equally, a call to tell them how much you appreciate the care that they are taking on the Mendips will also be welcomed.

BUS SERVICES

A number of bus services operate on the Mendips. Some are few and far between but in some villages there are regular services, and there are signs of improvement. For further information telephone Traveline on 0117 9555111 (8am–8pm daily) or First Badgerline on 0117 9553231 (8am–8pm daily).

INTRODUCTION
The Mendip Hills – a landscape of variety

To be on or around the Mendip Hills is to experience a landscape crammed full of myth, mystery and legend. Rich in history and diverse in aspect, this area has a quality unique in the south-west of England.

In 1972 the West Mendip plateau was designated an Area of Outstanding Natural Beauty (AONB) by the Countryside Commission. This designation, under the 1949 Countryside Access and National Parks Act, now protects 198 square kilometres of Mendip, stretching from Bleadon in the west to Litton and Chew Stoke in the east.

The Mendip Hills have always been recognised as extending beyond the boundaries of the AONB. The natural barrier of 'Greater Mendip' tradition-ally runs as far east as Frome; thus the area embraces a far wider variety of landscape than the uplands of the Mendips themselves.

Mendip is largely a farmed area. Drystone walls, a reminder of the enclo-sures of the late 1700s and early 1800s, criss-cross the plateau. Everywhere you look you will see the effects of centuries of human activity. It is a wild landscape, far harsher and more exposed than most people realize. It is also a delicate landscape that is vulnerable to damage; as such it needs to be treated with respect.

The Mendip Hills Warden Service has been operating within the AONB since 1983. The two full-time wardens are supported by over fifty volunteer rangers, who help with the extensive practical work, visitor contact and edu-cational activities for which the wardens are responsible. 'Enjoy but not destroy' is a message that is constantly being passed on to others who use the area. The wardens are normally the first point of contact for any problems or enquiries for locals and visitors alike.

A new Management Plan has been established to guide future work within the area. This plan will also seek to address various issues, such as development and tourism. The needs of the local community and wildlife conservation will also receive attention; this, after all, is a living and working area in which people are as much a part of the landscape as the open hills, drystone walls, woodland and hedgerows.

Being able to experience Mendip is a privilege for us all. We must all ensure that future generations can share that experience.

Les Davies,
Mendip Hills Warden

WALK 1
WESTERN BRACER

Christon – Shiplate Slait – Bleadon – Hutton Hill – Upper Canada – Christon

This western end of the Mendips, cut off as it is by the M5, has a character and atmosphere very much its own. It is windswept and bracing and yet receives the full benefit of the sun. It has the feel of the Somerset Levels as well as 'the Mendip moor' and there are memorable views.

SPECIAL INTEREST (see key on map):
1. Christon village and Christon church
2. Shiplate Slait
3. Bleadon and Bleadon church
4. Roman road
5. Hutton Hill
6. Upper Canada

Distance: 7.5 miles.
Map: OS Pathfinder 1197 Brent Knoll. Reference: 379 573. Also New Explorer 153.
Refreshments: Pub in Bleadon.
Terrain: Walking is on tracks and footpaths, through fields as well as on stony ground. It is likely to be quite muddy in parts after wet weather. Although the walk goes up and down the Mendips, it is very well graded and no uphill or downhill stretch should seem too long or hard.

START in the tiny village of Christon (**1**), which lies west of the M5 motorway, south-west of Banwell and north of Loxton. Christon can be approached from the Bleadon–Cross–Axbridge Road. If coming from Cross, go due west, over the motorway, turn right to Loxton and follow the road for about 1 mile to Christon. From Bleadon go east towards the motorway and then turn left to Loxton and along to Christon. From Banwell go down the small road at the side of Banwell Castle and follow the signs to Christon, crossing the motorway.

Find somewhere safe to park near the church.

11

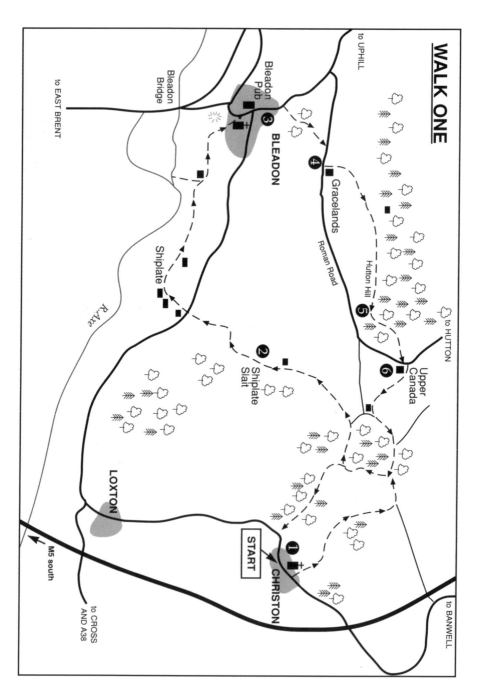

WALK ONE

to UPHILL

Bleadon
Pub

Bleadon
Bridge

to EAST BRENT

③ BLEADON

④

■ Gracelands

Roman Road

Shiplate

R. Axe

② Shiplate
Slait

Hutton Hill

⑤

⑥ Upper
Canada

to HUTTON

LOXTON

M5 south

to CROSS
AND A38

START ① CHRISTON

to BANWELL

Dennis Sleigh

Christon Church

If you like churches, this is one not to be missed. If only the motorway didn't drone away in the background.

(1) *This charming little church, shielded by ancient yew trees, is Norman though restored in Victorian times in the neo-Norman style. The carved south doorway has bold chevron mouldings within a huge stone porch. The lightness and humbleness of the interior, with its whitewashed walls, mellow-toned woodwork and simple carving, are striking. The window on the south side where the glass is clear in order to allow the sun in and the view of Crook Peak is a master-stroke. The church has interesting modern stained-glass windows. I particularly like the post-war memorial window on the north side, produced by a Bristol studio. The son, a bomber pilot, was killed in action on a raid on Kiel and is shown with a map of the German port. His mother was a VAD (member of the Voluntary Air Defence) in London – hence the searchlights and anti-aircraft guns in the background.*

Christon itself is now a small hamlet although there is evidence that the medieval village was much larger. Traces of old mine-workings show that at one time there was much mining here, probably for calamine and lead. The name Christon comes from the Saxon for 'place under the hill', the hill being Crook Peak (cruc is an old British word meaning 'pointed peak' or 'hill').

13

Take Flagstaff Road (merely a lane) at the side of the church and start to climb gently, continuing on as the track becomes grassy. As you climb don't ignore the beautiful view behind you across the valley to Crook Peak and eastward along the Mendip ridge. Go through a gate and then follow the track as it bends left. You can't fail to see the impressive stone boulders. Can you guess what they were for?

Chris Richards of the North Somerset Museum Service explained that these boulders come from a local quarry and were used to flank the drive to a nine-teenth-century shooting lodge, Barleycombe (which you may see in winter in the woods up on the right). The boulders are Dolomitic conglomerate of the Triassic period. The same rock – warm and pleasing – is used for roadside walls and buildings in the village. One of the guests at Barleycombe was Walter Raymond, the Victorian novelist who wrote Two Men of Mendip. *Barleycombe Lodge is where Lord Wainwright, the lord of the manor, invited his guests to shooting parties. When he was resident a flag was hoisted – hence Flagstaff Hill. Further up the field above the lodge there is evidence of medieval strip farming. These strip lynchets once covered a huge open area: after the Enclosures Act they were often parcelled up together and hedged around into separate fields, and then named.*

Continue up the track as it bends right to the top of the field. Go over a stile and walk straight on, keeping a fence on your right. Ahead is another magnificent view across Sand Bay to Wales and up to Clevedon and beyond.

You come to a crossing track – Bridewell Lane – a very ancient route along the Mendips as well as a parish boundary. Turn left and, at a junction of tracks, left again. At Keepers Cottage, turn right at the junction of paths. Go up to where a track marked 'West Mendip Way' goes left towards Loxton. Take this and continue climbing gently. Ignore the next track on the left; walk on up until you reach a gate. Through the gate, turn left into the field and take the path across it heading for the top of Shiplate Slait **(2)**.

On a clear day, here is one of the best views on the Mendips, and you really get that 'on top of the world' feeling, if the wind doesn't threaten to blow you over. You can see the top of Brean Down. Beyond is Steep Holm, the last and most westerly hill of the Mendips. To the south-west, left of Brean Down, can be seen Foreland Point, in Devon. There are good views south across the Somerset Levels and beyond as well as a panorama across Weston-super-Mare, Worlebury Hill, and up the Severn estuary. You can see how threatened this end of the Mendips is from the pressure of development around Weston.

Go through a gate and follow the path as it descends Shiplate Slait **(2)**. You will probably still see sheep grazing down here, which is appropriate as this was described as 'one of the finest sheep slaits [pastures] in England' at the end of the eighteenth century. The name 'Shiplade', meaning 'sheep-path', appears to date at least as early as the tenth century.

The path joins a metalled lane at a converted farmhouse and barns. With the Somerset Levels below, follow the lane down to the Loxton–Bleadon road at the foot of the hill. Go straight across and take the stile next to the cattle grid by Shiplate Manor Farm.

Cross the field diagonally to the far right-hand corner, heading for a stile to the right of the cottages. Bear right. Cross another stile and walk on, with a stream and farm buildings on your right and the magnificent Mendips as a backdrop. Come to a gate. Go right through the gate and left over a stile and continue on through flat fields, following the yellow arrows and heading for South Hill Farm up ahead. Go into the farmyard and, after a few yards, at a low stone building, turn right up a grassy track. Before the farmyard, you can go left down to the River Axe: this small detour leads to a good place for a riverside picnic.

The Axe rises about 20 miles away in Wookey Hole. Before the construction of tide-doors in 1802 where the bridge carries the A370 over the River Axe, the river was navigable for coal vessels and other small craft as far as Cheddar. It also had important fisheries but for a long time these were ruined by poisoned water from the lead works at Charterhouse and by chemical refuse from paper mills. Today, however, this stretch of river is again favoured by anglers.

The grassy track takes you up to a stile. Bear left up the field contouring the hill, with the farm down on your left, following the arrow. When you come to a junction of paths, turn right up the track heading towards Bleadon church. This will take you out of the field by an old quarry, down a path, through an iron gate and on down into Bleadon **(3)** to the churchyard. Turn left, passing the main door of the church (unfortunately, usually closed).

The noble tower of the church of St Peter and St Paul is conspicuous for miles across the Somerset Levels. There is a great sense of history here as a church has stood on the site since 956. The chancel, the oldest part of the present building, dates from the early fourteenth century and the carved stone pulpit is one of few surviving from such an early date: 1460. (You can read more about the church if you can get in.) The low window on the south side is a very unusual feature, whose precise purpose remains a mystery

Bleadon has had a few interesting rectors. One, Edward Powell, refused to take Henry VIII's Oath of Succession. His fate was to be hanged, drawn and quartered at Smithfield in 1540. He has since been recognised as a martyr by the Roman Catholic Church.

Leave the churchyard by a kissing gate and pass the old stone village cross, parts of which date back to the late fourteenth century. Turn right on the road, passing the hospitable Queen's Arms, a good stop for refreshment.

There is evidence of human habitation at Bleadon from a very early date. In 1997 six Bronze Age pits in which human bones dating from the Iron Age had been buried, were discovered. The site, earmarked for housing development, was carefully excavated and the finds taken away for detailed analysis. It was then filled in and the housing development went ahead as planned. Interesting DNA samples were taken from one of the skeletons ; it was of an individual, nicknamed 'Bleadon Man', who was 5 feet 8 inches tall and is thought to have died in about 150 BC, at the age of about 50. Comparison of the samples with DNA taken from local people revealed that a number of them were the descendants of Bleadon Man. West of the village, on the slope of Purn Hill, is the site of a Celtic field system. Bleadon was once a port on the navigable River Axe. In 1053 it belonged to Githa, wife of Earl Godwin and mother of King Harold. She gave it to the Priory of St Swithin at Winchester and thus the Bishop of Winchester was lord of the manor until the end of the nineteenth century. This affected the growth of Bleadon, which unlike many other villages, had no great house and family as its focal point but became a community of working people. All around was open sheep pasture, until the passing of the Enclosures Act in the late eighteenth century. The old part of the village (around the church) is built on mudstone and conglomerate of the Triassic period. Carboniferous limestone rises above. The village was never a centre for mining in the way that Shipham was, but there are signs of mining near the village on Hellenge Hill and Purn Hill. Most took place in the far north-east of the parish in the locality of Upper Canada Farm, where lead, calamine and yellow ochre were mined. A substantial cave system was discovered by the ochre miners. It was in this cave system that in 1757 Dr Calcott, a Bristol clergyman, and later, the Rev. David Williams of Bleadon and a local farmer known as 'Professor' Beard (famous for his discoveries in the Banwell Bone Cave) found remarkable fossils of large animals – some of them now extinct – such as wolf, tiger, cave bear, ox, horse and elephant. The route that our walk follows, between the stile on the path skirting the south edge of Hutton Wood and the road at Upper Canada, passes through the eighteenth-century ochre mines where the bone-cavern was found. The cavern was filled in after it was explored.

Continue uphill and at a bend leave the road and turn right on the public footpath (signposted to Combe Martin, Ilfracombe and Barnstaple when I walked here last!) A stile on your left brings you into a field. Cross the field and on the far side take the path leading into woodland. Follow it along and up steps and across another field, still climbing gently. The path brings you up to what is known locally as the Roman road **(4)**.

There is in fact no evidence that this straight road is Roman. It dates back to the 1788 Bleadon Enclosure Act. Enclosures were draughted on the drawing board; the resulting fields therefore generally have straight boundaries. This road was once a droveway along the edge of the straight fields. The field walls along the 'Roman road' are made of Carboniferous limestone quarried from small pits in the adjacent fields.

Turn right up the hill and shortly, just before a Gracelands, a very grand house on the left, turn left up the track following the footpath sign. At the end go over a stile. Bear right across the field and on to the crest of the hill. Crossing this field you view, to the left, the Bristol Channel and on a clear day Sugar Loaf Mountain and Pen-y-Fan, in the Brecon Beacons. Pass an old stone barn on your right and drop down to a stile. Cross the next field. Go over the track and take the path opposite, which continues on through the next field. Go over a stile and ahead along Hutton Hill **(5)**, with woodland on the left. Enter woodland at the end of the field, following a track. Cross a stile and continue on through woods and down to a lane at Upper Canada **(6)**. Turn left a short distance and, at the top of Canada Combe, turn right. Follow the track up to a T-junction of tracks at a cottage. Turn right up the hill and follow the track round, passing one footpath on your right and then another, which you took earlier on in the walk. Ignore this and continue, descending the hill. At a T-junction and cottage turn right and follow the lane downhill for about half a mile into Christon. Turn left along to the church.

A LINE INTO THE PAST

Axbridge – Winscombe via old railway line – Sandford Hill – Shipham – Winterhead – Fry's Hill – Axbridge

(shorter walk omits Fry's Hill and Axbridge)

This walk illustrates the varied human activity that has gone on around the edges of the high Mendip plateau. Railways, opening up wider horizons, had for all too short a time a great impact on the lives of the inhabitants of Mendip. This walk of contrasts and beautiful views follows one such railway line and then climbs gently up Sandford Hill, where there used to be quarrying. The route passes near a Roman villa, once a prosperous settlement, and the mysterious Wimblestone and goes on up to Shipham village – formerly 'a wild place' and hub of mining activity. Then on through beautiful rolling country, climbing up across two Mendip droves and onto Fry's Hill, where there are spectacular views. Head down to fascinating Axbridge, where again man made his mark.

SPECIAL INTEREST: (see key on map)
1. The old Cheddar Valley railway line
2. Shute Shelve Tunnel
3. Site of Roman villa
4. The Wimblestone – (not on a right of way so please ask the owner for permission to see it. Details at end of walk*)
5. Shipham village – once a centre of the mining industry
6. Peaceful Winterhead hamlet and evidence of mining
7. Nature reserve
8. Axbridge – church, square, King John's Hunting Lodge.

Distance: 8 miles, or 6 miles.
Map: Explorer 4, Mendip Hills West OS. Reference: 423 548 or (for the shorter walk) 419 560
Refreshments: Pub and shops in Winscombe; pub at Star; pub and cafe at Shipham; pubs and cafes in Axbridge.

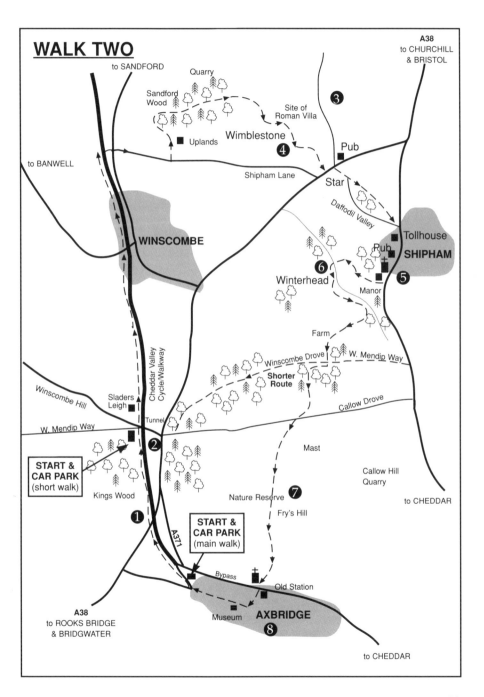

WALK TWO

Terrain: *The longer walk is quite challenging but well worth the effort. Easy walking over flat, dry terrain at the start is followed by some gradual uphill walking and one steep uphill section, with two downhill stretches (one quite long), which are not suitable for people with week or painful knees! The alternative, shorter route avoids the steep uphill and long downhill stretches. There can be some muddy areas, particularly on Winscombe Drove on the shorter walk.*

SHORTER WALK. Park in Kings Wood National Trust car park just off the A38 south of Churchill. From the north continue on the A38 through Sidcot, and just past a petrol station on the right turn right on Winscombe Hill. The car park is a short way along on the left.

To start the walk, go through the gate by the National Trust sign and then turn immediately left down a track, and shortly turn left on the smaller path which comes to a stile in the left-hand fence. Over, the stile follow the path down to the old railway line cycle/walkway **(1)**. Turn left and come to the railway tunnel. Follow the walk from *(See overleaf).

LONGER WALK. START in the public car park on the A371 Axbridge bypass just by the sign to Axbridge. If coming from the A38 from the direction of Sidcot, turn left towards Axbridge and the car park, about $^1/_2$ mile along, is on the right.

Pass between boulders on the other side of the small side road on to the old Cheddar Valley railway line **(1)**.

The Cheddar Valley Line was opened by the Bristol & Exeter Railway Company in 1869/70. It was the last line to reach Wells, providing a direct link with Bristol. In its heyday the line carried six passenger trains to Bristol a day , during the summer also serving Weston-super-Mare and Clevedon. It served the quarries at Sandford, Cheddar, Wookey, Dulcote and Cranmore and carried raw material for papermaking at Wookey. It also carried coal, cheese, milk and cider, and was nicknamed 'The Strawberry Line' because of the cargo of early strawberries, grown along the southern foot of the Mendips, that it carried. But, in the face of competition from road transport, passenger services were withdrawn in 1963 and freight in 1969. Thanks to the local authorities and much work by volunteers, the line is now a popular and expanding walk track and well-surfaced cycleway. It is also a haven for wildlife and much of it is a local Nature Reserve. You are likely to see blue damselflies, ox-eye daisies, yellow ragwort, marjoram and blackberries along the edges.

Follow the track, which offers fine views across the Somerset Levels and up

20

to Wavering Down. It soon curves round to the north amid bellflowers and vetch and many other wild flowers along the banks. Cross the A38 with care and walk on along the track on the other side, soon coming to the impressive railway tunnel **(2)** * (where the short walk joins). As you enter the tunnel you will be plunged into damp gloom: keep heading for the arched light and greenery at the far end.

Shute Shelve Tunnel was blasted out of solid rock in 1868. If you look carefully you may see the drill holes (now covered with moss) that were made to house the explosives. The northern part of the tunnel was lined with brick. During the construction of the tunnel many curious round 'potato stones', containing hollows lined with beautiful crystals, were found.

Approaching Shute Shelve tunnel from the south on the old Cheddar Valley railway line.

Shortly after emerging from the tunnel you may like to go up a short flight of steps on the left and look at Slader's Leigh **(3)**.

This is a narrow strip of meadow land managed by the Mendip Society, left when the railway was constructed. Because of its awkward shape it has never been ploughed or intensively farmed and is now one of the few remaining pieces of unimproved neutral/acid grassland sites in Winscombe Vale. Over 130 species of plant have been recorded, including devil's bit scabious, cowslips, betony, common spotted orchid and tormentil, as well as 21 different kinds of butterflies, and small mammals such as the yellow-necked mouse and dormouse. You can walk through the meadow keeping to the path.

Continue along the railway line past the site of Winscombe station, originally called Woodborough.

I always think of the story of the old chap in the village given the task of putting up the new station sign. He laboured all day to get the sign set up, but was too proud to admit that he couldn't read. Next day rail travellers were somewhat bemused by the new name of their station – [ɥƃnoɹoqpooM]! Winscombe was the village around the church and Woodborough was separate, providing the commercial and shopping facilities. The station name was changed because of confusion with the station at Woodborough in Wiltshire and gradually the old village name of Woodborough died out.

Continue on the path along the old railway line for a way, and stay with it as it diverts round gardens built on the old line. The main path descends a ramp, rejoining the old railbed, but you have to bear left up a smaller path to Ilex Lane. Go right over the bridge and follow the lane past houses. Cross the main Sandford/Winscombe road and take Shipham Lane ahead. Up on your left is Sandford quarry and Sandford Hill. After about 1/3 of a mile turn left up the drive to Uplands Cottages, heading towards Sandford Hill. At the bend in the drive, just before the house, go straight ahead on the grass up towards the woods. After entering the woods, turn left and continue along to a stony track and a cottage. Now turn sharp right on the marked path and follow it up through the woods. At a fork with an iron barrier, take the left branch. There are good views across the valley and up to Banwell Castle when the trees are not in full leaf. The path levels out and you pass alongside the boundary of Sandford quarry. Leave the woods through a gate onto a broad track and then take the stile ahead of you on the right.

The fields along the south side of Sandford Hill have long been famous for their flowers, insects and basking adders. The grassy areas between the trees here are honeycombed with old mine-workings for lead and calamine. Caves have been discovered on Sandford Hill and in one of them remains of a cave bear, cave lion and cave hyena – now in Somerset Country Museum,Taunton. It is also reported that in 1770 miners discovered the skeleton of an elephant deep in the hill.

Go straight ahead across the field and through the gap in the hedge. The path bears left and descends the hill via the waymarked post. There are great views south now across to Shipham and Sidcot and along the Mendips. Cross the track at the bottom of the field – often very muddy – and go over the stile ahead, then straight down the next field. The field on the left is the site of a Roman villa (3). Look for it when you are about halfway down the field, before you reach a small, heavily overgrown rectangular enclosure where a barn once stood. Look left into the next field back against the northern fence-line. You may be able to make out some grassy hummocks – the scarcely visible remains of the villa. The site is not on the public footpath.

The villa was sited near the old road from Old Sarum (near Salisbury) and near a reliable spring known as Pyle Well, a very important source of water for the area. Villagers from Shipham and its vicinity would have to carry water from the well quite long distance; special yokes were made so that children could fetch water before they went off to school. The villa seems to have been built on the site of an Iron Age farm. It was later rebuilt, and demolished around AD 350. It was clearly an important settlement. In 1826 diggings revealed underground passages – the remains of a hypocaust (underfloor central heating flues). Proper excavation was carried out in the 1950s and finds from the villa can be seen Axbridge Museum.

As you near the foot of the field you will see a rather wet area on the left and an oblong concrete structure: this is the site of Pyle Well.
The Wimblestone (4) is ahead of you in fields to the right but cannot be seen from the path. The landowner, John Horne, is willing for walkers to visit it if permission is sought from him beforehand. (To visit the Wimblestone and to find the best access to the stone, please contact John Horne on 01934 712242).

Many myths surround the Wimbelstone, one of the very few standing stones on Mendip, made of Dolomitic conglomerate. Its original purpose remains a mystery. Legend has it that the stone can move, or even dance, especially in the light of a full moon on midsummer's night, and that it can move about in search of water. Its name comes from the word 'wimble', meaning 'quick' or 'active'.

23

At the end of the field bear left, following the track which then bends right and comes up to the A38. Turn left. If you feel in need of refreshment, the friendly Star Inn is a few yards further on. To continue the walk, cross the road with care and turn up Cheddarcombe Lane, passing a line of what could be old miners' cottages (there was much calamine mining in the area). Go left over the stile. In the field bear right away from the left hedge and go up on to 'gruffy ground'. Continue to bear away from the bottom hedge. You get good views of Dolebury Hill Fort from here. Continue on up keeping the trees and Daffodil Valley on the right. (*The valley is so named because in spring it is a mass of bluebells and daffodils but a bridleway runs through it and it can be very muddy*). Go over a stile into a field/football pitch and walk on, keeping the trees on your right. Follow a path along and go over a stone slab stile onto the road in Shipham **(5)**.

Shipham, today a comfortable residential village, was once a poor and turbulent mining area producing mainly lead and calamine ore. The village developed rapidly in the eighteenth century, with individuals claiming their own mining rights on the commons (more than 100 mines for lead and calamine were record-ed in 1791). Around the mines grew a haphazard arrangement of cottages and narrow lanes. Calamine (a kind of zinc ore) was used in the brass-making indus-try. It was heated with metallic copper to produce brass. Records show that calamine mining began at Shipham in the late 1590s. It was exported to the lucrative brass industry on the Continent. When a brass industry developed in Bristol in the late 1730s, demand for calamine reached its peak and Shipham and Rowberrow were at the heart of the boom. Mining both for lead and calamine continued to flourish up to the mid-nineteenth century, with Cornish miners and others coming in to search for new veins. By the early 1870s the mining era in Shipham and Rowberrow had come to an end. For a while the miners sought work with the Mendip Mining Company at Charterhouse Mineries, walking the 5 miles to work along a track, which became known as 'The Slagger's Path', from the foot of Holloway up across Blackdown to Charterhouse.
In 1979 came the headline-hitting 'cadmium scare', with fears that the high level of cadmium in the soil could be harmful to health. An extensive test of the soil, water air, dust and plants, and of the residents, was made and ultimately the all-clear was given. Indeed, records show that villagers live to an age above the national average!
(The excellent Local History of Shipham, Rowberrow & Star Down the Ages, *produced by the villagers, is obtainable at local libraries.)*

Turn right, passing the old turnpike cottage, built when the road was turnpiked in 1827, and come to the Miner's Arms (still very much a traditional village pub) and Shipham village green. On the edge of the green opposite the pub is Lenny's Coffee Shop, a friendly community café run in aid of St Leonard's Church, serving reasonably priced snacks. (It is open all year round but closed on Sundays, Mondays and Saturday afternoons.) Continue along the main road past Penscot Farmhouse Hotel (the Shipham Inn until 1898) and come to St Leonard's Church.

It was rebuilt in 1843 and has an octagonal tower – rare in the West Country.

Pass the church. You are now at the bottom of Cuck Hill.

Cuck Hill takes its name from the 'cuck', or 'cock' horse – the third horse attached to a team pulling heavy loads.

Immediately past the church, turn right and pass a horse pond on your left and the old manor house on your right.

It is a traditional longhouse made of local stone and thought to have been built about 1380

Go into the field ahead and make for the far right-hand corner, ignoring any other exits. Cross a stile in the corner and walk straight on, keeping the hedgeline on your left and heading towards cottages in Winterhead, and passing just to the left of a telegraph pole.

The ground is very bumpy, further evidence of former mining. Up on the right is the only remaining mineshaft – now filled in and walled round for safety. It was sunk in 1869 in a vain attempt to restart the Mendip mining industry.

Head for the old stone barn and go through a marked gate onto a track in Winterhead **(6)**.

This is a quiet settlement with a number of attractive cottage conversions, and Winterhead Farm – the old manor house – approached by a tree-lined avenue. In the thirteenth century, part at least of the manor belonged to the Knights of St John of Jerusalem. It is said to be haunted by the ghost of the mistress of the house, who died under what were considered to be suspicious circumstances.

Turn left, following the stream and ignoring side paths, and start to walk uphill. Go over a stile into a field, then pick up the track and bear up left quite steeply. Over on your left are houses in Shipham and crowning them all is Daneswood House Hotel, once the famed Shipham Hydro, where homeopathic medicine was practised. Go through a gate and walk on straight ahead up the next field with a fence on the left. Go through another gate and right up the hill, hugging the hedge on the right. Pause for breath to enjoy spectacular views across the Sidcot valley to the Severn estuary. At the end of the field cross a stile and head across the field towards Winterhead Hill Farm. A gate brings you onto a track. Turn left and follow this to the junction with the West Mendip Way. Turn right.

SHORTER WALK: Stay on the WMW (also known as Winscombe Drove – one of the old tracks across the Mendips), going gently up along the edge of Winterhead Hill (the summit is up on the right). Keep straight on – don't turn right. Then start to descend gently. After about 1 mile, where the track can be muddy, join a concreted track (the end of Callow Drove). Turn right and continue down to the A38 opposite a garage. Cross carefully, using the island, and turn left a few yards and then right into Winscombe Hill and to where you started.

MAIN WALK: After a few yards on the WMW take the first gate on the left, climb up the field steeply and pick up a track leading up through the wooded gully. At the top bear slightly right across the field and go over a waymarked stone slab stile onto Callow Drove. Cross into the field opposite and head for the far right-hand corner. Callow Hill ('Bare Hill') is a magnificent vantage point, now somewhat spoiled by the Mendip radio masts, but much more significantly by the huge workings of Callow Quarry to the east of the masts. Go over the stile and ahead up the field, with the hedge on your right. Go over another stile and walk on downhill, following the stone wall and shortly go over a stile in the wall on the right. It is often very muddy here, due to the trampling of cattle. Continue on down steeply through the nature reserve **(7)**.

Mining for yellow ochre was once carried out on the hill, with a simple rail system to take trucks up and down the incline. The ochre, which was used as a pigment, was processed at Cheddar, on the Axe.

Go over a stile at the foot of the reserve and straight ahead down the track heading for Axbridge churchtower. Look out for concrete steps on the left. Go down to the Axbridge bypass. Over on your left is old Axbridge Station, with patterned roof tiling and decorative bargeboards. Cross the bypass carefully, go slightly right and then left away from the road across the rough ground which was part of the station, heading for the church. Take another flight of steps. Then turn right, down more steps and left down into Axbridge **(8)** and to St John's Church above the fine square.

It sits in a commanding position in the town and has a noble tower. Inside, the roof is a particularly outstanding feature. Axbridge is a fascinating town which once had a reputation as a health resort, especially for people with consumption. However, Axbridge Church Registers show that the town suffered several fatal epidemics including outbreaks of plague and smallpox. The fertile soil and the sunny southern aspect made its market gardens famous for early produce, including strawberries. To learn about the history visit Axbridge Museum, housed in King John's Hunting Lodge, on the right of the square. (It is open from Easter to September, 2pm to 5pm, and admission free. It is not, as the name implies, a former hunting lodge nor does it seem to have any connection with King John. It was built as a house in the sixteenth century and once consisted of four shops with storage and accommodation above.

Continue up the narrow street at the side of the museum. Keep straight on at the junction, with Compton House on the left. Then cross and take the small road heading for Weston-super-Mare with a cycleway marked at the side. The car park is at the top on the right.

DRAMATIC DOLEBURY

Burrington Combe – Mendip Lodge – Dolebury Hillfort – Rowberrow – Black Down – Burrington Combe

This walk begins with Burrington Combe and north-facing woodland. The route then passes the ruins of an extraordinary, extravagant mansion and climbs up to dramatic Dolebury, where the views can be quite magical. The route then runs downhill and across to the hamlet of Rowberrow before taking to shady woodland and then on to Black Down for the final downhill sweep.

SPECIAL INTEREST: (see key on map)
1. Burrington Combe
2. Ruins of Mendip Lodge
3. Dolebury Hillfort and Warren
4. St Michael and All Angels at Rowberrow
5. Rowberrow Warren
6. Black Down and swallets

Distance: 6.4 miles
Map: Explorer 4 Mendip Hills West OS. Reference: 477 587
Refreshments: Restaurant in Burrington Combe; The Swan Inn at Rowberrow
Terrain: This is a walk of reasonable graded ups and downs – with one steep climb down steps. It is mainly on woodland paths and tracks and open grassland. There is one section of woodland which can get muddy, so be prepared

START in the public car park in the beauty spot of Burrington Combe (1), near the garden centre and restaurant, and to the right of the public toilets. Burrington Combe is on the road running south across the Mendips from the A368 Churchill – Blagdon road. Turn right out of the car park and pass the cafe and garden centre.

The restaurant was a small wood building put up in 1927 by Mr Roynan of Burrington Farm. The main house was built in 1934 and hundreds of tons of

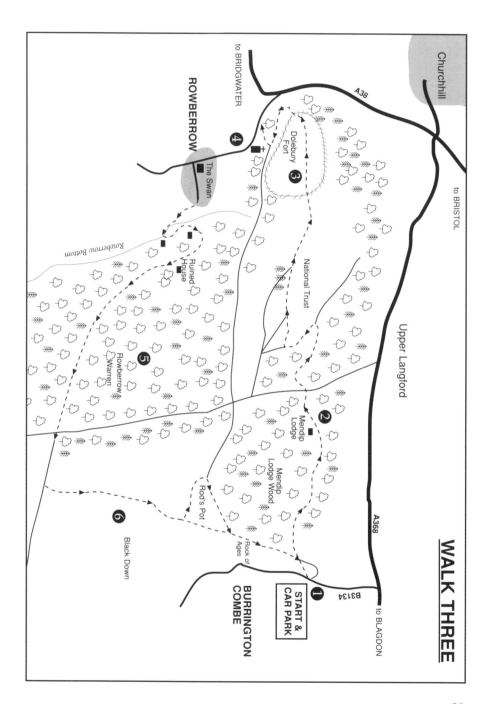

WALK THREE

Churchhill

to BRISTOL

A38

Upper Langford

A368

to BLAGDON

B3134

START & CAR PARK

BURRINGTON COMBE

Black Down

Rock of Ages

Rod's Pot

Mendip Lodge Wood

Mendip Lodge

National Trust

Rowberrow Warren

Ruined House

Rowberrow Bottom

ROWBERROW

The Swan

to BRIDGWATER

Dolebury Fort

29

stone brought in to level the ground and fill the 12-foot gully in front of the restaurant. The garden centre was established in 1967.

At the garden centre, cross the road and take the slip-road opposite. Along this, just before a cottage, take the marked public footpath which climbs steeply up the slope and joins a small road. Turn left and shortly take the marked path on the right. Go into the woods, following the yellow arrow along a stony path uphill. Continue along a clear path in the wood. Since tree clearance this path offers goods views over Wrington Vale. It is a pleasant wood, but much invaded by laurels and rhododendron ponticum (evidence of a former magnificent garden). After about $^{1}/_{2}$ mile you reach substantial ruins of an old house with stone walls and the outlines of window shape – Medip Lodge **(2)**.

What remains of Mendip Lodge is no more than a decaying shell, giving just a hint of past glories, some say follies. The Lodge was begun by Dr Thomas Whalley in 1787. He was a clergyman with a reputation for lavish hospitality and generosity. According to Vincent Waite, in his book The Mendips, *Dr Whalley married the heiress of Langford Court, a wealthy widow, somewhat older than himself; they lived happily together despite the fact that he proceeded to reduce her very considerable fortune by his extravagance. Ten years later, such was the state of his finances that he was forced to let Langford Court, and it was then that he began to build Mendip Lodge. Apparently it began as a modest cottage, but took on grander proportions. A friend wrote: 'It is the loveliest architectural luxury I ever saw.' Built in the Italian style it boasted an 84-foot-long verandah, a 'noble' dining room adorned with fine pictures, a state bedroom fitted out in anticipation of a visit by the Duchess of York, and perhaps most remarkably 'the painted rooms in which landscapes in trellised frames had been painted on the walls, apparently by some French prisoners who were drafted into Bristol during the Napoleonic wars'.*

The terraced grounds were something to behold and included beautiful woods, and park-like and finely timbered pasture land sloping down to the road below. Another visitor was less impressed, describing Mendip Lodge as, 'a show place in which a vast deal of money had been sunk upon two follies'. After the death of his first wife, Dr Whalley married another wealthy woman. She died two years later and, according to Vincent Waite, 'the widower spent the next eight years squandering the remainder of her fortune'. The choice of a third wife was less propitious and they separated after a while. Dr Whalley's life ended in sad decline. In an attempt to put his finances right he tried to sell Mendip Lodge, but a house reputed to have cost a fortune – £60,000 – failed to realise £30,000. He died, aged 82, while visiting France. After a period of neglect, then restoration, Mendip Lodge also began a steady descent from the giddy heights envisaged by Dr Whalley until it is what we see today.

Continue past the old house on the main drive and, as it sweeps away down to the right, go straight ahead, following a small path to the right of the ruined old stables. At a T-junction, turn left up a stony track. Walk on for a couple of minutes then go right over a stile into land owned by the Woodland Trust. Take the path left up the hill. Near the top of the slope you come to a crossing path. Turn right here and continue on for a while. The woodland on the left gives way to open fields. When you reach a gate and stile on your left, make an about turn. Go over the stile and up the field in the direction of the footpath sign, keeping a line of trees on your right. At the end of this line of trees, walk on in the same direction across the field. There are lovely views over Wrington Vale. Go over a stile and along a track with planted woodland on the left. After 150 yards you reach an open sward on your right, running to the top of Dolebury. Head up this slope and continue on. In late spring and summer this area is covered with a wonderful selection of limestone grassland wild flowers. Follow the Limestone Link waymarked sign. After a few minutes you reach the eastern outer banks of Dolebury Hillfort **(3)**.

Here's a place where the imagination can truly take flight. Enjoy it and respect it: it is a Scheduled Ancient Monument and Site of Special Scientific Interest. The eastern approach to the hillfort over which you have just walked was its weakest point: hence the double line of ramparts and what was probably an outer defence. You have also just crossed, although you could be forgiven for not knowing it, an ancient Celtic field system. Little detailed work has been done on the history of Dolebury, but it is said to be an Iron Age hillfort looking out over the Somerset Levels. The main gateway, at the western end, was defended by a triple row of mounds and ditches. Along three sides of the hillfort there is a double line of defences, but because to the south the hillfort overlooks a steep ravine, a single wall on that side was judged sufficient.

Roman and Saxon coins, spearheads and swords have also been found on the site. Stand on the highest point and take in the strategic views. To the north is Wrington Vale; to the south, the broad plain; to the West the Bristol Channel and the Welsh Hills.

As Frances Knight somewhat fancifully put it, 'Garrisons of Dolebury may have watched Roman war galleys putting in at the mouth of the Axe; may have watched the sea-fight that drove the pirates of Brittany over to the coast of Wales; may have witnessed the landing on Steep Holm of Githa, the mother of King

Dolebury Hillfort from the air

Harold, with all the ladies of her train, in the year after the Battle of Hastings.'
More mundanely, Dolebury has also done service as a rabbit warren, providing
food for the local people. Keeping rabbits was a serious business. Within the hill-
fort was a warrener's house, more than twenty vermin traps (covered runs
ending in a trap, often a stone box or pit) and and some eight 'pillow mounds',
artificially constructed to encourage the rabbits to burrow and breed within the
hillfort area. As you walk across the centre of the hillfort, it is still possible to
make out what is left of some of the larger mounds, running north to south. Like
other areas of the Mendips, Dolebury has periodically been the subject of mining
operations for iron, lead manganese and calamine.

Continue on the path through the centre of the hillfort. You may see the
remains of the old warrener's house, in ruins by about 1830, and now just a
collection of stones on a raised mound with the vestiges of some walling.
When the grass is high the path may not always be easy to make out; just
keep straight on across the centre of the fort, enjoying wonderful views. You
will eventually come to the other (western) side of the fort and another raised
bank with the opening for what was the west gate. Go left up onto a small
path on the top of the the bank and follow it along to the south-west corner

of the hillfort. From here you can look across to the village of Rowberrow and its church. That is where you are heading. Then drop down a few yards ahead and slightly right on a small path, and look for the start of a path that goes right, descending many steps to the foot of the slope. This is not a good section of the walk for people with weak knees! Take it easy and use the wooden bench conveniently placed halfway down. Continue down the steps and over the stile into the parking area.

Here, a small information board makes it clear why Dolebury Warren remains important to this day. English Heritage has designated it a Scheduled Ancient Monument, and English Nature has listed it as a Site of Special Scientific Interest. It is a ridge of limestone heath with flower-rich grassland. The flowers include bee orchids and pyramidal orchids, yellow-wort, dropwort and kidney vetch and there are some thirty species of butterfly.

On entering the parking area, turn left, go over a stile, and follow the wide track, which is also a bridleway and often muddy. After about 320 yards, having passed an old corrugated shed on the right, turn right onto a small footpath (by a gate marked 'private') which climbs up to the road into Rowberrow. In early spring a mixture of wild garlic, anemones and bluebells decorate the way. Turn left along the road and head for the church.

The church of St Michael's and All Angels, Rowberrow (4), stands on a site where Christians have worshipped for 1300 years. The present church, however, dates back only to 1865, although the Perpendicular tower was built in the early fifteenth century and only the turret and pinnacles were replaced in 1865. Among special features, the church has a ring of six bells cast in 1752 by the famous bell-founder, Thomas Bilbie of Chew Stoke. Next to the south porch of the church is a memorial to Thomas Venn, who in 1812 was 'Crushed to Death' in a mine when he was just eighteen years old.
Rowberrow, like Shipham, was a calamine-mining centre in the eighteenth century. Also as at Shipham, the calamine (and lead ore) was found in vertical or steeply dipping veins running through the Dolomitic conglomerate. In 1791 it was recorded that fumes from the calamine ovens were killing vegetation. Rowberrow was also the scene of unsuccessful deep-mining trials in the latter half of the nineteenth century. It is worth noting the setting of the church next to the manor house and the warm and pleasing use of the local conglomerate for roadside walls.

Leave the church and continue along the lane into Rowberrow and to the popular Swan Inn. Turn left along School Lane and go downhill to some pretty cottages sitting alongside the stream. The track to your left would take you past the remains of calamine workers' cottages, but cross straight over into the clearly signposted Rowberrow Warren (5) and head uphill following the bridleway signs to Blackdown. It is a fairly long haul, but there are opportunities to stop and enjoy the view. Ignore a track on the left, but at a junction of tracks pause to enjoy the splendid views across to Wales – a truly beautiful spot on a clear early evening with the sun setting on the Bristol Channel. Go left for a few yards and you will see the ruins of the warrener's house, but your actual route lies to the right and then almost immediately left, onwards and upwards, along the bridleway to Blackdown. There are a number bridleway signs to give reassurance, but if in doubt continue on upwards in the same direction. In spring, in the more open areas, there is likely to be a fine show of foxgloves. Eventually you emerge onto Blackdown (6). There are many tracks on Blackdown, some of them churned up by horses, making the going rather confused and sticky. Your direction is fairly simple. Continue on the bridleway until you meet a large crossing bridleway. There, turn left and head downhill towards trees, enjoying the views over Wrington Vale as you go. Shortly before you reach the trees ahead, turn left onto another marked bridleway. This is, in fact, a small detour which runs alongside Rod's Pot to another bridleway, where you turn right and continue with the trees on your left.

Rod's Pot may look like nothing more than a depression in the ground, but the junction at which you are now standing is in a line of Mendip swallets: running west to east, they are Reads Cavern, Bos Swallet, Drunkards Hole, Rods Pot and Bath Swallet. **Don't be tempted to explore these holes. Caves are very dangerous places.** *Read's Cavern is a typical Mendip swallet but with the distinction of having been occupied in the Iron Age. This occupation was brought to a close by a massive rockfall. When cavers first entered in 1919, the main chamber of the cave was strewn with signs of occupation – pottery, metalwork and hearths. The depression at the entrance of Bos Swallet was used in the Early Bronze Age by Beaker people as an occupation site and later, in the Middle Bronze Age, as a meat-boiling site.*

Why are the swallets here? Water cannot penetrate the old red sandstone which caps Black Down. It flows off this and across the lower shale until it reaches the carboniferous limestone. Here it penetrates, exploiting and widening the cracks and crevices which are a feature of the limestone. Water swallowed by Read's Cavern emerges at Rickford and Langford as springs.

The track you are on eventually turns into a made-up road. Go down the hill and you will recognise the start of the walk. Watch out for the little steep footpath on you right on which you came up at the start of the walk (or just simply follow the lane down) and reach the road by the garden centre, restaurant and car park.

If you failed to notice it before, look across the road from the car park to the Rock of Ages. (see page 39 for details).

DISCOVERING BURRINGTON

Burrington Ham – Burrington Hillfort
– Rickford – Blagdon – Burrington Ham

(shorter walk omits Blagdon village.)

*This adventurous circuit (with two alternatives), which in parts
follows some fairly unknown and little-used paths in the heart of
the Mendip Area of Outstanding Natural Beauty, brings out the
glory and some of the history of the northern edge of the plateau,
and explores the last big open space on Mendip – Burrington Ham
Common, which extends over more than 1,000 acres. Visit a little
explored hillfort, learn the true story of the Rock of Ages, see
evidence of former mining. Explore pretty Rickford, which used to
be a flourishing hamlet centred around its mill, and fascinating
Blagdon village. For a spectacular sight of bluebells in late
spring, take the slightly shorter alternative route, which
passes through a picturesque bluebell wood.*

SPECIAL INTEREST: (See key on map)
1. Burrington Ham
2. The Rock of Ages
3. Burrington Hillfort
4. The Bowl
5. Remains of mining
6. Rickford
7. Blagdon village

Distance: Full Walk A: 5.5 miles; Walk B: 5 miles
Map: OS Explorer Map 4. Mendip Hills West. Reference: 489 581.
Refreshments: The Plume of Feathers pub in Rickford; several pubs in
Blagdon
*Terrain: Walking is on grassy tracks and footpaths and lanes, and is a mixture of
flat, downhill and uphill walking – with one fairly long uphill, but gradual section
out of Blagdon (particularly on walk A), but the views are excellent. There are a
couple of sections where you walk quite close to the edge of Burrington Combe so
make sure that your footwear has a good grip and keep children close to you. Please
keep dogs under control throughout this walk as they may disturb the many deer
which lie up in this whole area.*

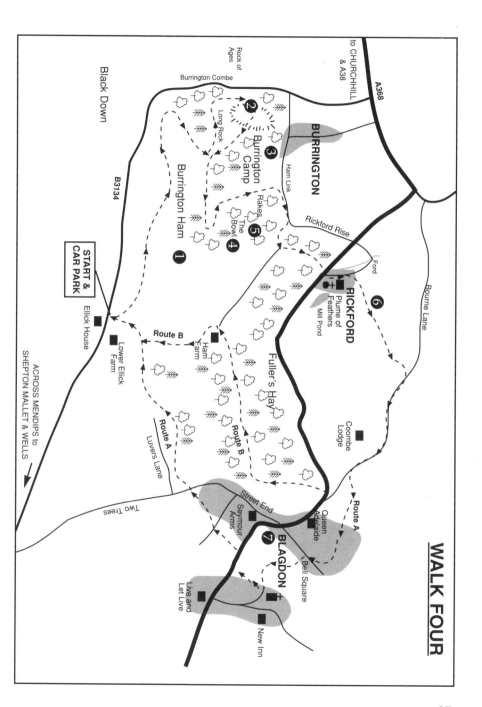

WALK FOUR

37

START in the car park near the top of Burrington Combe on the B3134, giving access to Burrington Ham. This relatively small parking area can get rather crowded so you may have to park somewhere safe nearby. (It won't be long before you leave all the other sightseers and walkers behind.)

Take the main rocky path at the back of the car park (in the back left corner if facing the car park from the road.) Come up onto Burrington Ham Common **(1)**.

If you look carefully you may see bumps and ridges up here. These are the remains of Celtic field systems. Much clearance work is being carried out here by the Mendip wardens as part of a ten-year plan under the Countryside Steward-ship scheme to improve the quality of access, to halt the invasion of scrub and to restore the former patchwork limestone landscape with its characteristic flora. The work will involve clearance of scrub and some trees and rebuilding of walls, and low-intensity grazing will be reintroduced by bringing in some Exmoor ponies.

Shortly turn left (west) on the broad, grassy track following the footpath sign, and not the bridleway straight ahead.

Along here, as in many places on Mendip, you may see some silvery-black galena cubes which contained the lead, as well as yellow ochre in the soil. The low grassy bank on your right is the remains of a boundary of an old field system. Along here you pass hollows and long crevices in the ground, evidence of the former lead and calamine mining that was carried on here.

The path branches – and you can go either way. The paths come back together again to form one track, which then again divides. (You can choose either route.) Fifty yards after the paths rejoin for the second time you will see a deeper hole on the left with a ladder (if it is not too overgrown). This was left by cavers in the 1970s and the pit is now sealed up. Just past this, look for a small but quite well-defined footpath going left at 90 degrees. Follow it across towards the edge of Burrington Combe.

From this sunny vantage point you can see up across Black Down to the highest point on Mendip, Beacon Batch, as well as west to Wales and north to Clevedon and beyond. Follow the edge carefully along with the combe down on the left and come to the top of the Great Scarp, which rises steeply from the road along the bottom of the Combe. Continue to follow the edge until you can safely go no further and then take one of the paths going right (north) down the hill and then across the more cleared area and up to Long Rock – another wonderful vantage point, this time facing north across Wrington Vale. As another walker aptly put it once when I was here, 'sitting here makes you think that God must have been an Englishman!' Walk along this rocky ledge, keeping Wrington Vale down on your right, and follow the path as it bends down to the left. Stay on the path as it narrows and winds through bushes and small trees (it may be quite overgrown in parts), avoiding side turnings. Before long you will come back to another part of the steep edge above Burrington Combe. Then the path bends right, with the combe edge still on the left. When you can go no further along the edge, the path goes down right through the trees. Be careful as the path is uneven and rocky in parts and soon comes up to a small clearing and the combe edge again. Across to the left there's a great view of the cleft of the famed Rock of Ages (2).

The widely believed story that the hymn Rock of Ages was written by the Rev. Toplady, curate-in-charge at Blagdon, when sheltering from a storm in the rock's cleft has since been officially debunked by the Hymn Society of Great Britain. It appears that he wrote the hymn years after leaving Blagdon, where he was in fact curate for only two years from 1762. He was in London preparing his next sermon, and needed a hymn to accompany it, so he duly produced one. Toplady's sermon was based on the rock that Moses cleaved. His choice of words was influenced by the words of a seventeenth-century Dean of Durham which appeared in Wesley's Sacramental Hymns (the words were not by Wesley himself). The hymn has no connection with the crevice in Burrington Combe. Of course, it proved much more colourful when promoting the Combe to visitors to imagine the rector writing this dramatic hymn in recognition of the shelter it gave him!

Follow the directions carefully here as the route is not well walked. Continue on the path for 15 yards and turn right onto another small path (if you reach rocky steps you have missed the turn). After another 12 yards the path forks. Go left and follow it for a couple of minutes until you come to the outer ditch of Burrington Hillfort. Go over this and after 20 yards fork right on a small path through trees and come to the open area of the hillfort (3).

Burrington Hillfort's origin and use remain something of a mystery. Expert opinion differs. It may date from the Iron Age, although its small size could suggest it may perhaps be Bronze Age. Some archaeologists conclude that there is no evidence whatsoever of any occupation. Excavations carried out just after World War II unearthed no finds suggesting occupation. However, in his book The Heart of Mendip, *Francis Knight refers to a find made early in the nine-*

teenth century of a bronze dagger with gold hilt set with turquoise, and in 1910 the Rev. R.H. Edwards of Burrington found a Neolithic flint axe. It seems as though the camp was built hurriedly, perhaps against a threat that never materialised or which came so fast that the site was overrun before it could be completed. Whatever secrets it retains, it is a beautiful, peaceful spot.

To continue the walk go across the hillfort bearing slightly right. Exit over the outer ditch on the far side. Keep on in the same (easterly) direction through another cleared area. Long Rock ridge, which you visited earlier, is up on the right. You may just glimpse it through the trees in summer. Bend round on the path to the right at the end of Long Rock and come up to the main path. Turn left down the hill, taking care, as it can be quite slippery. Continue down for a few minutes to the foot of the hill. Ignore a path going off to the left. Continue through a slight dip, which is often wet and muddy. When the paths forks, take the left fork and almost immediately turn left on what is the reinstated bridleway. But before continuing along the bridleway, turn right and walk a few yards down through trees; you will find yourself looking north across an area called The Bowl or Hill House Gardens **(4)** where a plantation is growing up.

This was a market garden area, where potatoes, vegetables, soft fruit and fruit trees were grown in the nineteenth century. The fertile, well-watered soil, the sun and the shelter from prevailing winds made it an ideal spot for cultivation.

Return to the bridleway. Follow it along with Hill House Gardens down on the right and continue on down. At a more open area you can see grassy hillocks and long deep depressions. These are rakes, where miners followed seams of minerals **(5)**. To see more and clearer rakes, go up to the right, but beware of getting lost: return to the path at this point.
To continue the walk, follow the rocky path down to a crossing lane – Ham Link. Turn right and keep on to a junction. Turn right and very shortly bend round to the left (avoiding a track going up on the right). Pass a shed on the right and start to go uphill, and after a few yards turn left on the bridleway into woodland. Follow it all the way down to the road above Rickford, avoiding a path going off to the left. Take care when you join the road at this dangerous bend. Turn right and cross the road towards impressive Mill House, with its waterfall and lake alongside.

This was once a millpond serving a flourishing flour mill and later a paper mill. The flour mill in Rickford appears to have been destroyed by fire. The paper mill, built in the late eighteenth century produced good-quality paper and later artists' papers. Paper was still made by hand there until 1895. The lake is fed by the main Rickford Rising not far away and by a secondary spring. The small church, originally a Baptist chapel, is now a masonic lodge. The Mill House, was probably built in the reign of James I.

Go left down the small road into Rickford **(6),** passing the attractive turreted Victorian gauge house whereby Bristol Water controls the stream from the lake. It gravitates by a pipeline into Blagdon Lake. Pass the welcoming Plume of Feathers. It's easy to spend time here idling by the water or sitting in the sun outside the pub or up in the garden behind.

Rickford is a picturesque spot where the clear waters of the stream support water crowsfoot, watercress and yellow monkey musk, which grows along its edges.

Dennis Sleigh

Gauge house at Rickford.

Walk on through the hamlet. The walk proper continues by taking a right turn opposite the red brick building on the left; it was built as a workshop and used as a carpentry shop, builder's yard and store until it became a flourishing painting centre (now moved elsewhere). However, before you take this path you may like to go on to the end of Rickford and see the ford and beautiful old Brook House at the side. (Down by the ford there appears once to have been a tannery.)

To continue the walk go up the steep and narrow footpath opposite the brick building. At the top you will see that it is called The Stocking. (The origin of this name unknown.)

This small path was once known as Leg Lane and the lane that runs up behind the pub and joins it at the top was originally called the Stocking. For some reason, when the lane and path were officially labelled the names were changed over– and Leg Lane also acquired another 'g'! One old man who lived in Rickford all his life said it was now the wrong way round because the stocking should be bigger than the leg!

At the top turn left past cottages and at the end go over a stile and straight across three fields with Wrington Vale over on the left until you come out through a gate onto Bourne Lane. Turn right and continue on the lane for about $^1/_2$mile, past Ridge Farm and with a good view up to Blagdon Lake appearing. Continue along the back of Combe Lodge, one of the last substantial country homes in England.

This large mock-Tudor mansion with many gables and mullioned and transomed windows was built in 1932 for Sir Vernon Wills on the site of an old Georgian house. In recent years the house has been leased to the Further Education Development Agency; since this organisation has decided to relocate, the future of the house is uncertain.

Continue on, passing some of the buildings put up as part of the Combe Lodge Estate.

Built in the style favoured by Lord Winterstoke – stone, half-timbering and plasterwork – at the beginning of the century, they included the Home Farm, the Agent's House, Head Gardener's House, Dairy, Laundry and the Engine House. Happily many of the buildings have been converted into workshops for light industry, keeping the area alive.

On your left, rising up from the dip in the road, you see two stone estate houses with a drive between leading to garages. It is at this point that you can decide whether to take Route A – the longer way through Blagdon – or Route B.

For the shorter walk, Route B, turn to page 45

MAIN ROUTE A: Go left and take the footpath between two of the garages. You'll soon get a good view down to Blagdon Lake and the fine Victorian pumping station with its two magnificent beam engines (occasionally opened to the public by Bristol Water).

Blagdon Lake was formed at the turn of the century by damming the River Yeo and flooding 450 acres of farmland. It is now renowned for its trout fishing. The dam was built in eight years almost entirely by hand with much labour coming from all parts of England and Scotland. Blagdon is a village that was significantly affected by two things – tobacco and water. The Wills family (of tobacco fame) came to the village as lords of the manor, bringing with them wealth and the lure of plentiful employment. Later Blagdon Lake attracted tourism.

Follow the path go through fields and kissing gates until you come out onto the edge of Blagdon **(7)**. Follow the residential road to the end. Ahead is Walnut Tree House

Once a very simple dwelling, this now quite substantial house shows the old tradition of extending a house for a newly married son and his wife. This happened twice at this house. When the original walnut tree died it was replaced by a new one and among its roots was buried a bottle with details of life at the time; unfortunately, the top came off and the papers rotted. The present walnut tree in front of the house was planted in 1985 – again with a bottle among its roots containing sociological information
The name Blagdon may come from the Anglo Saxon 'Black Done', meaning Bleak Down – an apt description when the north-easterly winds sweep along this edge of the Mendips.

Turn right and at the junction turn right up the lane, and after 200 yards turn left into Bell Square.

The Bell Square Preservation Society successful campaigned to save the black iron hydrant when Bristol Water threatened to remove it. The square contains some of the oldest cottages in Blagdon, dating from about the fourteenth century.

Take the footpath on the far side of the square which links the two halves of Blagdon and gives wonderful views across the vale and lake. Follow the path across towards the church, passing Tim's Well.

This was one of only two water supplies for the village and was restored to mark the Queen's Silver Jubilee in 1977. Carrying full buckets of water from the well up the hill and home must have been a strenuous necessity for the inhabitants of Blagdon.

Come up to the entrance to the church. Its tower – over 116 feet high – is one of the tallest in the country and the fifth-highest in Somerset. Inside, the church is filled with light and colour. It is worth a visit, but is not always open.

The first church, built in 1317, has long since disappeared. The present building dates from Victorian times. The church has figured strongly in the life of the village. In the mid-eighteenth century the evangelist Hannah More was at the centre of a row over Sunday schools. While she and the evangelical branch of the church were in favour of Sunday schools, the conservative faction considered them to be dangerous Methodist propaganda. This 'Blagdon Controversy' focused considerable attention on the parish.

If you feel in need of refreshment, the New Inn is a couple of minutes' walk away: leave the churchyard at the far side, head along the road and at the end you will see it down on the left. There are other good pubs in Blagdon including The Live and Let Live, on the main road, and the Seymour Arms, also on the main road but further back in the village.
To continue the walk, turn right on the grassy path just before the church. Come out onto the road. Turn right, passing a 'communal orchard' – Eldred's Orchard – on the right.

There's a lovely story about this orchard. The original land was given to the village council by an anonymous donor with the proviso that the corrugated iron shed in the field should be kept there and maintained – the reason being that it was here he used to do his courting! Sure enough, you can still see the rusty shed down the bottom of the field. The trees are owned by individual villagers and each January there's a popular wassail by way of celebration.

Cross the road with care and then go left up a small marked path, the Grove. Pass a converted Methodist chapel on the left. Follow the path up to the junction with Street End Lane at the top. This is the boundary of the old medieval village.

The rule was that outside the boundary it was possible to put up an overnight house on any scrap of land available under the tradition of the 'overnight hearth'. In one day a prospective cottager built up the walls with turf or any rough material and then built a rough inglenook and topped it all with a simple roof made of poles and turf. Once the fire was lit in the hearth, the builder claimed ownership and could then set about making it a more secure home. Many families were brought up in cottages like this, many of which, like Rock Cottage, have been converted out of all recognition.

Go straight ahead up the steep rocky path by Rock Cottage to some modern garages and follow the path straight ahead to the left of the garages. At the top is an open picnic area at Blagdon Rocks – a magnificent view and rest point. Bear left across the grassy area and turn left on the road.

Opposite is the old Mendip Hotel – now offices. It was built as the Mendip Bungalow with corrugated iron roof and asbestos walls before World War I. It developed into the Mendip Hotel, a popular venue where people came from considerable distances to enjoy tea and tennis. What a spot to choose!

After a few yards turn right on the marked footpath (a metalled driveway) on the bend. Go up the grassy track and through a field gate. Go ahead, slightly left across the field, keeping the wire fence to your right. Once again you can feel the wind on your face and enjoy the views. Go through the marked gate in the hedgeline ahead and cross the next field bearing diagonally left to the top hedge. Follow the hedge keeping it on the left and then go through the gate onto Burrington Ham common. Turn left down to where you parked.

ROUTE B: Continue on Bourne Lane a few more yards and turn right up a steep, short stone track by a small building used by the gas authorities.
At the top cross the main road with care. Follow the yellow arrowed path opposite for a few yards, then turn left up a small path to a stile into a field. Go up the right-hand side of the meadow with the woods on the right and go over another stile into the next field. (In order not to disturb pheasant and deer, dogs should be kept on a lead in these fields and in the woodland to come.) Continue on up to another stile and then bear right following the arrow across the next field to a gate in the corner. Go straight across the next field to stile rails by a gate. Walk on straight ahead with the woods on your right and then enter beautiful Fullers' Hay, where the sunlight filters through the trees, highlighting a carpet of bluebells in late spring.
Follow the path through to a track on the other side of the woods and bear right. This takes you out to farm buildings. At the end of the stone barn on the left, turn left up the track to a stile into a field. Bear diagonally left up across the field to the far left-hand corner. Go into the next field and then up the field with the hedge on the left. Go over a fence/stile. Aim for the far right top corner of this field. The official right of way is straight up the left side and then right along the top hedge line. This brings you to a gate in the corner through which you re-enter Burrington Ham common. Turn left through trees to the parking area.

THE HEART OF MENDIP

Charterhouse – Blackmoor Reserve – Beacon Batch – Longwood Nature Reserve – Velvet Bottom

(Shorter route omits Beacon Batch)

Hard though it is to imagine, this rural backdrop is the setting for a walk into Mendip's industrial past. The Romans settled here, drawn by the area's potential for mining lead. Picture the scene: a Roman fort, a settlement, probably an amphitheatre representing a small but significant part of the Roman Empire. Down through the ages, others, such as the Bishop of Bath and Wells (1189) and the Carthusian monks of Witham Priory, in the thirteenth century, continued the mining here. It was not until the seventeenth century that mining activity reached its peak. After that there was a lull, followed by a period of reworking waste material, and some deep-mining in the nineteenth century. Moving closer to our own time, what is an air raid shelter doing close to the highest point on Mendip? And then there's natural history. This area is at the heart of the Mendip Hills Area of Outstanding Natural Beauty.

SPECIAL INTEREST: (see key on map)
1. Charterhouse Centre
2. St Hugh's church
3. The Romans and lead-mining
4. Later mining
5. Blackmoor Nature Reserve
6. Sites of Roman occupation
7. Highest Point on Mendip
8. World War II 'Decoy City' and air raid shelter
9. Longwood Nature Reserve
10. Velvet Bottom and more reminders of lead mining

Distance: 5.75 miles or 4.5 miles.
Map: Explorer 4 Mendip Hills West OS Reference 501 555
Terrain: *This interesting walk has uphill sections (short but steep in one place) and stretches of downhill walking. Walking is on footpaths across fields and along quiet*

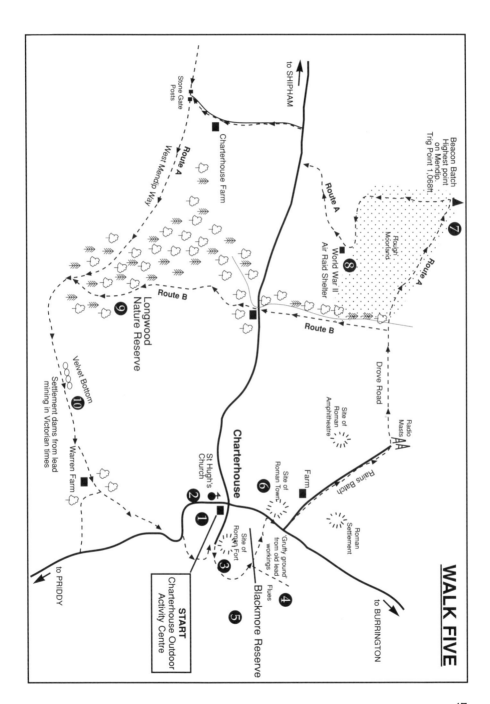

WALK FIVE

to SHIPHAM

Beacon Batch
Highest point
on Mendip.
Trig Point 1,068ft.

Stone Gate
Posts

Charterhouse Farm

Route A

West Mendip Way

Route A

World War II
Air Raid Shelter

'Ffudgi'
Moorland

Route A

7

8

Route B

Route B

Drove Road

Longwood
Nature Reserve

9

Site of
Roman
Amphitheatre

Radio
Masts

Rains Batch

Velvet Bottom

10

Settlement dams from lead
mining in Victorian times

Warren Farm

Charterhouse

St Hugh's
Church

2

1

6

Site of
Roman Town

Farm

Roman
Settlement

to PRIDDY

Site of
Roman Fort

3

'Gruffy ground'
from old lead
workings

Flues

4

Blackmore Reserve

5

to BURRINGTON

START
Charterhouse Outdoor
Activity Centre

47

roads and lanes. For the longer walk up to Beacon Batch, footpaths can be muddy, particularly in winter.

START at Charterhouse Outdoor Activity Centre. To get there, take the B3134 road across the top of the Mendips from Burrington Combe to Wells and Shepton Mallet. Go all the way up Burrington Combe and after about 4 minutes you will see a road marked to Charterhouse (on your right if coming from Burrington – on the left if from Wells). About 1 mile along this road you will see the activity centre on the left by a crossroads. Park in the car park on the far side of the centre.

The centre **(1)** was once Charterhouse village school. It closed in 1947 and the centre has developed as the leading Mendip information resource, concerned with educating and informing the public. It is also the home of the Mendip Warden Service. You may like to call in to look at the displays, pick up leaflets or walk cards (of which this walk is a variation) or chat to one of the wardens. Although it is likely to be locked, the church **(2)** on the opposite side of the road is interesting.

The church is dedicated to St Hugh, one-time Prior of Witham, to whom Charterhouse once belonged. The name Charterhouse also relates to the monks at Witham: they were Carthusians who came originally from Chartreuse in France – the monks and place which gave the world the famous liqueur, Chartreuse and Charterhouse its name. The church itself is the work of the Rev. G. M. Lambrick and the architect W. D. Caroe. Lambrick, a curate based in Cheddar, agreed to accept the living of Blagdon on condition that he could 'take Charterhouse with him', having it officially transferred to Blagdon and that he be given permission to build a church at Charterhouse. Caroe systematically rebuilt the old miners' welfare hall on the site, leaving only the fireplace in the north wall and the scullery at the west end. The cross which stands close to the road is inscribed 'March 7, 1909', the date of the consecration of the church, and 'To the glory of God and in memory of those who lived and worked on Mendip and who lie in God's acre beneath the hill'.

Leaving the church, head back towards the centre, passing it on your right and taking the first turning to the right at the crossroads. A little way down the lane stop at the gate on the left and look into the field. This is the site of the Roman fort.

(3) *The Romans were mining lead on Mendip in* AD *49, just a few years after the* *conquest. Indeed it may have been the promise of Mendip lead that originally brought them to the area. Lead was subsequently shipped across the Roman Empire, beginning its journey on one of the network of Roman roads on Mendip – mainly along what has become known as the 'Lead Road' , east across Salisbury Plain to Winchester and on to a port near present-day Southampton. Another road headed west to Uphill, the River Axe and the Bristol Channel, and there was a link to Sea Mills on the River Avon, but it seems clear that the main route was eastwards. The Romans used lead for a number of things, including plumbing – the Roman baths at Bath are lined with Mendip sheet lead – as well as for pewter, to make vessels and platters – some of which were made at Shepton Mallet and Camerton – and for lead coffins. Mendip lead is even reported to have been found in Pompeii.*

Continue your walk by entering into the small car park area. The walk takes you left but first go ahead in the car park, over a stile and along a footpath for a few yards.

Here on the left are the barely visible, ground-level foundations of stables and the site of the Pattinson Plant. With the lead came small quantities of silver, and the Pattinson Plant was designed to separate the one from the other. In 1865 the workings yielded 326 tons of lead and 1,300 ounces of silver. Around here, there are small quarries which give sight of the nature of carboniferous limestone, with its veins, bedding, planes and fossils.

Return to the main route and follow the track along and through a single-bar gate, ignoring the track which branches to the right. Continue for about 300 yards, ignoring for the time being a side path. At a junction of paths, keep a post marked 'S' on your right, and continue on a few yards. Then bear right to a wire fence and a post marked '6'. Here are what look like stone tunnels but which are, in fact, horizontal flues used in smelting (4). (*The posts, erected by the Mendip Warden Service, are part of a special interest and wildlife route.*)

Lead was mined on Mendip before the Romans came and after they left. The peak of production seems to have been in the first half of the seventeenth century. Mining was organised into liberties administered by four Lords Royal of Mendip – the Bishop of Bath and Wells, and Lords of Harptree, Chewton and Charterhouse – who received 10 per cent of any ore mined on their land. The miners had a special status and lived under special laws, which among other things involved 'throwing the hack'. To measure the length of this claim, a miner stood in his groove up to his waist and threw the hack or pick in either direction

Dennis Sleigh

Flues at Charterhouse.

along his rake, or vein. The miners worked along these veins close to the surface, leaving behind them grooves – what is called 'gruffy' ground. When these seams began to run out, the mining industry went into steady decline. In the nineteenth century the industry received a new lease of life. About 1860 the Mendip Mining Company set up a smelting works – reworking waste material left by earlier generations of miners. The waste material was washed in large pits known as buddle pits, where revolving arms kept the material moving. The heavier lead-rich substances gathered in the centre and then went for re-smelting in the furnaces. The resulting liquid lead was run off into moulds and cast *into blocks, known as pigs, while the smoke from the furnaces, heavy with lead vapour was conducted through stone galleries – like the flues you are looking at – where it condensed into a solid deposit on the walls. From time to time this was chipped off and resmelted. It is said that poor boys from the Wells workhouse were used for this dangerous work. The diggers and furnace men came mainly from Shipham using what is still known as the Slaggers Path.*

Natural History

With industrial history comes a particular natural history. The area you are in is the Blackmoor Nature Reserve **(5)**, owned and managed by Somerset County

Council, and the woodland near the remains of the Victorian condenser flues is Nether Wood. (There is a wheelchair-accessible trail.) The woodland contains streams and ponds, which is unusual on Mendip as water normally drains quickly through the Mendip limestone, but here the underlying shale provides an impervious layer, effectively allowing the miners to hold water necessary for the lead-mining process. The trees are mainly ash and beech. In spring there are daffodils and ramsons (wild garlic); in summer wild raspberries grow close to the track. Generally there are plants associated with lead, including alpine pennycress and spring sandwort. The area is noted for its butterflies. It is also a good place to see buzzards and kestrels. Fox, badger, hare, stoat, weasel and roe deer can sometimes be seen. Adders and lizards like the dry grassland. If left alone adders are unlikely to cause harm. Care should be taken, particularly near walls.

Now retrace your steps for a couple of minutes. (*Notice the glassy lead slag left over from the resmelting.*) Look out for a marked path going right which leads across the wet land and on over a small wooden bridge, across a stile and up through a field to the road – all in the space of a few hundred yards. Ahead is Town Field and here and all along the hillside were once Roman settlements **(6)**. Turn right along the road and after about 160 yards turn left up a road marked 'No Through Road'. This is called Rains Batch. Continue quite steeply up it towards the radio masts. Near the top, over in a field on the left, is a circular earthwork, believed to be the site of a Roman amphitheatre.

Evidence of Roman life at Charterhouse has been unearthed by the more recent mining activity. Among the finds were jewellery, locks, keys, spoons, tweezers, hair pins and coins plus many pieces of Samian pottery – so called because it was made on the island of Samos.

At the radio masts, turn left on a track known as Drove Road, which passes between fields and heads straight for the highest point on Mendip, Beacon Batch, rising to 1,068 ft **(7)**, on Blackdown. The down is formed of old red sandstone of the Devonian period Just before you reach the end of Drove Road and come onto the open land of Blackdown, there is a footpath which goes left over a stile into the field. This is the short walk (Route B) see page 54.

LONGER WALK, ROUTE A:
This continues to the Trig Point on Beacon Batch, which you will see on a clear day as you approach.

From Blackdown there are superb views across the Bristol Channel. Closer by, amid the undergrowth you can still make out lines of overgrown long peat mounds constructed during World War II to look like the outlines of buildings when viewed from the air and dim lights were lit at their ends. This 'Decoy City' **(8)** *was designed to mislead German bombers and originally stretched from Charterhouse in the east to Shipham in the west. There are also Bronze Age round barrows near the Triangulation Point.*

From the Triangulation Point follow the Mendip Warden footpath sign (black, white and red waymark plaques) left, down to the hedge line (this sign is often missing!). In winter this stretch can be very sticky. Turn left and proceed to the building on the right, a World War II air raid shelter.

The shelter was used by the men lighting the decoy fires. Presumably, if they were successful, they would have had bombs raining down on their heads!

From here cross into the adjoining field and backtrack on yourself at an angle of about 45 degrees following a bridleway sign. Follow the bridleway into another field and head for a track in the bottom corner which links the field with the road. Turn right on the road and, after 200 yards, left down the drive to Charterhouse Farm. (If you would like a little extension go past the turning to Charterhouse Farm and shortly on your left you will see a gate to land managed by the Somerset Wildlife Trust.)

This is known as GB Gruffy. It is a large swallet complex and cave system of national geomorphological importance. It has neutral to acid species-rich grass-land and lead/calcareous exposures. Access to the caves is by permit only, but you are permitted on the land.

Having headed down the drive to Charterhouse Farm, at the bungalow bear right, follow the track out across the field and up to a gate with large stone posts. Before the gate turn left along the West Mendip Way and follow it along, and eventually steeply down through the edge of Longwood Nature Reserve **(9)**.

Longwood Nature Reserve is leased from Bristol Water by the Somerset Wildlife Trust. It is one of the very few examples of ancient woodland on this part of Mendip with evidence of broadleaf trees going back to the thirteenth century. Now the wood is managed, with the aim of restoring its wildlife and original mix of ash, oak, field maple and sallow. A nature trail gives access to the wood, which is probably at its best in spring with wood anemone early on and the smell of wild garlic later: bluebells and red campion provide contrasting colour in May. And everywhere, there's the sound of birdsong as the birds claim their territories. Butterflies, foxes and badgers are just a few of the other inhabitants of Longwood, which also contains evidence of the area's geological origins.

Cross the stile and follow the defined track for about 100 yards, bringing you to a point where Velvet Bottom joins Black Rock Drove. Go left through the wooden gate at the side of the stone slab stile. (Route B rejoins walk at this point.)

** **BOTH ROUTES:** Follow the path alongside the wall, then right, up the steep hill and stay with it as it winds up and bends back left. Then continue on. At times the path may be unclear, but you want to gradually bear up right towards the boundary fence/wall at the top. There is no hurry. This is quite a long section of the walk. You just need to keep roughly on in the same direction but making for the top and then follow the boundary – making sure you do not cross. You are walking with good views, high up above Velvet Bottom (**10**).

Velvet Bottom is another nature reserve owned by Bristol Water and managed by the Somerset Wildlife Trust. It is on the floor of a dry river valley much influenced by lead workings and is a Site of Special Scientific Interest because of its ecology and archaeology. Reminders of lead mining can be seen in the shape of the now grassed-over settlement dams of Victorian times. These are said to have been designed to retain lead and stop polluted water entering the water system. There are very few trees because of the lead in the soil but the dry grassland supports populations of adders and lizards. On a sunny day butterflies and grasshoppers add to the beauty of the area and there are foxes, stoats and weasels. A variety of flowers helps complete the picture as the year progresses, though some will need to be looked for – the yellow flower of coltsfoot; early purple and common spotted orchids; lady's smock; hogweed; spear, marsh and creeping thistles; and in early autumn a few patches of heather.

Continue along the top boundary. Cross a stile in the fence ahead of you and go straight across the field with the woodland and Warren Farm over on the right. Go over another stile ahead and follow the footpath sign right along the fence line with the wood over on the right and arrive at the track to the farm. Turn left along the track to the road. Turn left along the road for about 5 minutes ignoring stiles on the right into Ubley Warren, and at the sharp left bend go right through a marked small wooden hunting gate and along the path. On the left of the path nature has reclaimed the spoil of Roman times, on the right are the remains of more recent workings. At the road, turn left and walk up to the junction and the Centre.

SHORTER WALK (ROUTE B)

Take the footpath, left from Drove Road. It is about one field short of the open land of Blackdown. Continue down the fence line through the field and come to the head and then along the side of a pretty little valley called Blue Bell Valley – massed snowdrops in March, massed bluebells in May. Go over a marked stile and just continue on in the same direction and eventually come out over a stile onto a road by houses. Turn right and almost immediately left on to a footpath which crosses a small stream and then goes alongside it for a short while before bearing away. Follow the path across to a line of trees, through a band of woodland and over a stile. Then go up hill into a field and ahead following the edge of the field. Bear right across the corner of the field to a stone stile in the wall ahead. Cross over and continue on with the wall on your left until a track joins from the left. At this point go diagonally right across the field you are in, down to the far corner and another stile. Cross and continue alongside a stone wall, and cross another stile. Go straight ahead in the field and then bear slightly right and enter the trees and bushes down a distinct 'throughway' which goes downhill. When you come to the open space at the wall at the foot, turn right, over the stone wall and into Black Rock Nature Reserve. Go left immediately through the wooden gate on left and rejoin main walk **.

IN AND AROUND THE GORGE

Wells – Underwood Quarry – Ebbor Nature Reserve and Gorge – Wookey Hole – Arthur's Point – Wells

This walk, starting on the edge of Wells, soon leads you into peaceful countryside, climbing fairly gently to the open heights of Mendip. It follows the beautiful Ebbor Gorge Nature Reserve, with one of the best vantage points in Somerset. Some may choose the more rugged route, descending the Gorge itself; others can enjoy the gentler paths of the nature reserve. The route passes through interesting Wookey Hole village and finally reaches Arthur's Point. This walk offers many opportunities for stopping, so allow plenty of time.

SPECIAL INTEREST: (see key on map)
1. Underwood Quarry
2. Ebbor Gorge and Nature Reserve
3. Wookey Hole – village, mill and caves
4. Arthur's Point

Distance: 5.2 miles
Map: Explorer 5 Mendip Hills West OS. Reference: 542 463
Refreshments: Pub and cafes in Wookey
Terrain: A slow, steep uphill climb near the start is followed by a good flat stretch of walking, and a descent through Cheddar Gorge (or a bit of a climb down). After this the walking is quite easy, on footpaths and tracks, although there is one potentially wet and muddy area as you leave the Gorge. Make sure that you have sturdy footwear with good grips.

START on the northern outskirts of Wells, just north of the Blue School. Park in Ash Lane somewhere suitable near the footpath which runs each side of this wide residential road. *Coming from the direction of Bristol and Bath* take the A39 down the hill nearly into Wells and then turn right on the road marked to a business park and Wookey Hole. This brings you into Ash Lane. Or come down the Old Bristol Road over the Mendips from Hunters Lodge and

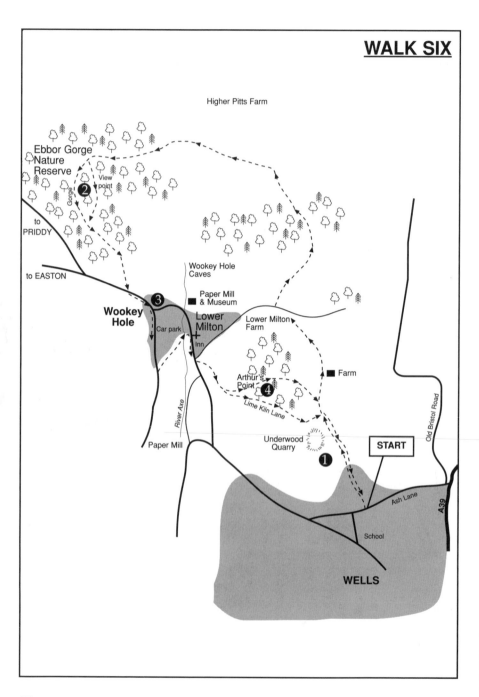

WALK SIX

Higher Pitts Farm

Ebbor Gorge
Nature
Reserve

View point

Gorge

to PRIDDY

to EASTON

Wookey Hole Caves

Paper Mill & Museum

Wookey Hole

Lower Milton

Car park

Inn

Lower Milton Farm

Farm

Arthur's Point

River Axe

Lime Kiln Lane

Paper Mill

Underwood Quarry

START

Old Bristol Road

A39

Ash Lane

School

WELLS

56

Priddy. Drop down the hill on the edge of Wells and turn right into Ash Lane. Ignore Milton Lane and Fir Tor and look for footpath signs on each side of the road. This is the West Mendip Way which crosses at this point.

Coming from Wells, go along the bypass towards Bristol and Bath. Go left on the Wookey Hole road at the traffic lights. Take the first right – Kenyon Road – up past the Blue School. At the top, turn right in Ash Lane and park near the footpath signs on either side.

START the walk by taking the footpath on the north side of Ash Lane going uphill on a dring (narrow path between houses). Cross a road and keep on up. Come out through a kissing gate onto an open area. Keep straight ahead still climbing gently and picking up the old quarry track. Due to possible subsidence you will need to leave this shortly. Go right over the stile – thanks to the work of the Mendip wardens – and left in the field following the left hedge and keep on to another stile which brings you back onto the track alongside the quarry.

This footpath from Wells to Wookey Hole has been fought over and saved by local people on more than one occasion. When it was threatened in 1895 Wells' citizens, armed with pitchforks and scythes, marched behind the town band along this right of way and demolished the barriers that the landowner had erected. In 1949 there was another campaign by local people, this time led by Herbert Balch, Wells' famous postmaster and local historian. It was against the proposal to divert the footpath in order that Underwood Quarry, then owned by Somerset County Council, could be extended, virtually wiping out much of the hill behind. Local feeling seems to have won the day.
Underwood Quarry (1) ceased operations around the 1970s and is now used by various light industries. In 1936/7 a rift was found in the quarry and in it were buried dirt and bones. These were identified as being the bones of 150,000-year-old hippopotamus, deer and some bovine animals. They are now in the care of Wells Museum.

Ignore left and right turns. Just keep straight on, ignoring the farm road on the right, and take the marked footpath through a kissing gate into the field ahead. Bear right down across the field to the left of the farm. I love this particular view of fertile rolling English countryside crowned by the bare slopes of the Mendips. Go through a kissing gate by the farmhouse and down the field ahead and over a small stream, through a kissing gate and follow the path gently uphill with the hedge on your left. At the top of the ridge bear away from the hedge and cross the field. Leave it through another kissing gate and climb gently up across the next field to the top left corner and out onto a lane over a stile.

Turn left and after a few yards come to Lower Milton Farm cottages. Opposite the drive to the cottages go right through the second metal gate and ahead along the hedge. A gate at the end brings you into another field. Follow the left-hand hedge, climbing steadily all the time. Go through a gate into another field and continue on up as before. The rocky outcrops in these fields in this area yield a pretty selection of wild flowers.

At the top go ahead through a marked gate into woodland onto a stony track.

This was almost certainly the track that was used for bringing minerals and iron from the Mendips down to Wells.

Follow the track ahead, uphill for about 10 minutes, enjoying the changing views. Go through a gate and into a field and head straight up the hill and then bear across to the left hedge line. Cross a stile and continue ahead, following the hedge.

The land around here and nearby Higher Pitts Farm was worked during the nineteenth century for short periods by various different small prospectors and companies for a variety of minerals, notably manganese, and for iron.

This is a wonderful stretch of the walk, with tremendous views on the left and the feel of the wide open spaces of Mendip. Keep straight on. Cross one stile and eventually you come to a waymarked wire fence ahead of you. Turn left along it, passing a rocky area, remains of former quarrying. Cross a stile into Ebbor Gorge **(2)**, passing 'a run-off dewpond' on the right (constructed so that water naturally runs off from the hill above into the pond). Go over another stile and onto the main stony track down through the beautiful mixed woodland. Please stay on the paths as it can be dangerous if you stray and keep dogs on a lead in order to avoid disturbing the roe and barking deer and other wildlife.

In Ebbor Gorge, you can see a great variety of trees, such as dogwood, wayfarer, wild privet and spindlewood. The dampness makes it an ideal home for many different ferns, mosses, liverworts and lichens, including some rare species. Ebbor Gorge was formed during the Ice Age and there was evidence in the caves of the gorge of animals, such as reindeer, lemming and red deer, which lived here during the extreme cold.

According to achaeologists, the Gorge was once a vast cave, the roof of which was gradually worn away over millions of years. On either side of the gorge there are many small caves and rock shelters. Don't try and enter them as it could be dangerous and they are important homes for colonies of bats.

There have been many finds showing that man inhabited the huge Wookey Hole Cave and other caverns in this area as early as 60,000 years go during the Pleistocene period and continued to dwell here for many thousands of years. Neolithic stone tools were found, as well as artifacts and human remains dating from the Bronze Age, when the caves may have been used as burial chambers. The Gorge area was given to the National Trust by the Hodgkinson family – responsible for the development of Wookey Hole village – in memory of Winston Churchill. Today it is administered by English Nature.

Come down to a cross of tracks in the Reserve. There is a choice to be made here, but beforehand it's worth going along to enjoy one of the most spectacular views in Somerset from a rocky prominence called Ebbor Slaits. So follow the red arrows towards the car park for a few minutes until you reach a cliff-edge warning sign. Go out to an open area and you find yourself at the top of the cliff with tremendous views across the gorge and across the Somerset Levels. It is south-facing and so can be very warm here – but it can also catch the full force of the winds.

The choice – those who would like to see the full drama of the gorge and are steady on their feet might like to go down the gorge itself on a steep path which goes down through the ravine, or you can follow the main reserve path which goes more gently down steps to the same point.

ROUTE 1 – GORGE WALK: Retrace your steps for a couple of minutes to the crossing tracks and then go down left on the path. It's a spectacular walk but go carefully as you make your way down through boulders and rocks and through the narrow pass, the Split. One can easily imagine Stone Age people making this ravine their stronghold home. Continue down passing a dramatic scree slope on the left and further on noting the polypod ferns on the trees. This area is particularly beautiful when the sun filters down through the trees. At the bottom keep straight ahead, ignore the path on the right to the car park and the path on the left where Route 2 meets up. Continue from **

ROUTE 2 – EASIER ROUTE: Simply continue to follow the car park red arrows and come down to a crossing track at the foot of the Gorge and then turn left and join up with Route 1 from **.

** Everyone now is back together. Follow the path through the bottom of the gorge. Go over a stile leaving the nature reserve and head along a narrow grassy valley. Come out through the wicket gate at Kennel Batch. Turn left on the lane passing attractive Ebbor Hall on the right – one of the oldest houses in the village, parts of it dating back at least 300 years and on the left Ebbor House, which was originally a cottage.

The name Wookey is of Celtic origin. It means a hole or cave, in other words the famous, huge cave which is set into the dramatic rock behind the village and which, along with other caves, is open to the public. The cave was renamed Wookey Hole to distinguish it from Wookey, when the village of that name grew up just a short distance away. Many of the cottages in Wookey Hole are made of the local stone of Dolomitic conglomerate known as 'pudding stone' because it is made up of a 'pudding' of ingredients – sandstone, limestone or quartz pebbles mixed together with a red mudstone.

Turn right and go up this lane, passing a number of country homes on the right and heading in the direction of the paper mill chimney at Haybridge. Go left through a wooden gate into a grassy open air car park and across to the River Axe as it merrily starts its journey, having just risen from the ground at Wookey Hole.

The village owes its existence to the River Axe, which rises deep under the Mendips and emerges near the entrance of the cave. The abundance of trout, pike, crayfish, loach, flounder and other fish provided a good source of income for the bishops of Bath and Wells, and the fresh and plentiful supply of water was the reason for the establishment of the paper mill.

Turn left along the river through what has become a picnic area and overflow car park – very attractive out of season. Just as you reach the main car park you can turn right over a small bridge and come up to the road in the village by the Wookey Hole Inn. Or you may choose to go on to the cafe and refreshment kiosk in the car park, or if you have time, visit famous Wookey Hole caves and paper mill.

For centuries the mill has been at the heart of Wookey Hole village (3). It was a corn mill and also a cloth mill but went over to handmade papermaking in 1610. It is the only surviving mill of its kind in Somerset.
The mill today produces a limited quantity of fine handmade paper, using old rags rather than wood pulp. There is an interesting exhibition on papermaking

60

at the mill and you can have a go yourself.

The old mill was destroyed by fire in 1855 and a new mill built. During this work debris and bones were discovered in a small cave, the Hyena Den, and proper excavations then unearthed relics dating back thousands of years. In the big cave many priceless treasures have been found, many of which are in Wells Museum, and which show that the cave was lived in from about BC 250 . During excavations in Badger Hole bones of prehistoric horse – the forerunner of the Exmoor pony – were discovered.

The first known record of Wookey Hole big cave was that of Clement of Alexandria in the third century AD, showing that the cave's fame had spread abroad even then. The caves have attracted visitors on a small scale for many centuries. Then, in 1927 a concerted effort began by the Hodgkinson family to attract more visitors. Electric light was installed and stairways built. The entrance was widened, and a woodland walk made leading to the entrance. In 1935 there were more improvements with a car park, restaurant, museum and swimming pool. During World War II the buildings were occupied by the army and the ATS.

Madame Tussaud's brought their expertise to bear when they ran the whole concern from 1973-1989 and then sold it to a couple of local businessmen.

Exploration and discoveries of new caverns still continue, thanks mainly to the courage of intrepid cave divers.

Wookey Hole before 1848 was a very quiet peaceful village, with its mill, a few cottages and one or two larger houses and farms and an inn. The seeds of the present village were sown in 1848 when a London gentleman, Mr W.S. Hodgkinson, decided to buy the mill and land in the village. During the next thirty or forty years he and his son built the greater part of present-day Wookey Hole. Mr Hodgkinson built houses for the mill workers and a fine new school, which opened in 1872 with ninety children. For himself and his family the second Mr Hodgkinson built a handsome residence, Glencot, on the site of an older house with gardens, a cricket ground, tennis courts a bowling green and four staff houses. It remained in the family until it was sold in 1927, and after several changes of use, is now a luxury hotel. You can see Glencot and the paper-makers' cottages set above the village to the side of the mill.

Whatever you choose to do, go to Wookey Hole Inn and pass it on your left. There are tea rooms and café for snacks on the right with a terrace overlooking the river. Pass a chapel on the left. Ignore the first turning left and shortly at a bend go left through a wooden kissing gate on the West Mendip Way. Go ahead up onto the raised bank, following the right hedge. Go through a kissing gate and along a path. Go through another gate and here you have a choice of routes to get you to some magnificent limekilns.

ROUTE A: – the shortest. Go ahead to another gate and turn left on the lane (Lime Kiln Lane). The lane is a lovely place in spring with banks full of cowslips. Follow it until you see an opening on the left to the lime kilns. These are very well preserved and unique in the area for being three together. Behind the kilns is a quarry cut into the hill by Italian POWs during the last war. Follow the West Mendip Way signs in front of the kilns. Go through a band of woodland and then across a more open area and straight on along the main path. A stile brings you back onto Lime Kiln Lane with Underwood quarry ahead of you. Go left and immediately left again following the WMW into the woods. Ignore side paths and stay on the small main path through the woods, dropping down to a crossing path. Go right on the WMW to the junction where you came earlier on this walk. The quarry is on your right. Now retrace your steps, * taking the stile on the left into the field, along the hedge line to another stile and back onto the lane. Then straight ahead, across the open area and down the dring to where you parked.

ROUTE B: This is much steeper. Turn left up the field going up on to the ridge, staying on it with a band of trees on the left, and keep going until you reach woodland. There is a stile ahead. Go through onto a path. Up ahead on the hill is Arthur's Point.

The point was a good lookout for the early cave dwellers. It's name may be connected to the many legends of King Arthur, which abound in this area of Somerset. However, it could just as easily been named after one of the men who did the looking out! Numerous weapons and relics from the Bronze Age have been found on Arthur's Point (4).

You can now either: 1. Make your way steeply up to the top of Arthur's Point and over, down the steep descent to the path going into woodland; or , 2. Follow the path round the left-hand edge through woodland. The path bends round the hill and along the far side and into woodland. (Here you meet up with anyone going over Arthur's Point.) Follow it along and out of the woods into the top of a field (down in the far corner is the Model Farm you passed earlier). Go straight along the top edge, out of the field and onto the lane and retrace your steps from near the start of the walk*.

HARPTREE COUNTRY

Harptree Hill – Smitham Chimney – East Harptree – Harptree Combe – Harptree Hill

This walk explores the lower northern slopes of the Mendip escarpment, yet is high enough to capture the feeling of Mendip isolation, open spaces and great views. It was on the slopes that the settlements grew up and where much of the history of former generations is to be found – such as at the stronghold of Richmont Castle, and the old cockpit above West Harptree. The circle also passes by an amazing Victorian feat of waterworks. Higher up there is much evidence of former mining, and the only remaining smelting chimney on Mendip. The circle also explores an enchanting Mendip combe. Although spring, when bluebells are out, shows the area at its best, it is beautiful at all times of the year. It would make a good early morning or late afternoon walk (of about 3 hours), ending with refreshment back at the starting point. There is also a pub along the way.

SPECIAL INTEREST: (see Key on map)
1. Site of an old cockpit
2. Remains of mine workings
3. Smitham Chimney
4. East Harptree church and village
5. Harptree Combe
6. Site of Richmont Castle

Distance: 5.5 miles.
Map: OS Explorer Map 4. Mendip Hills West. Reference: 545 560
Refreshments: Pub where you park and in East Harptree.
Terrain: The walk is a good balance of uphill, flat and downhill walking – none of it extreme. The main uphill stretch is at the end. It runs along footpaths through woods, fields and quiet lanes. Alongside the stream in beautiful Harptree Combe it is often very muddy and wet, so go suitably shod.

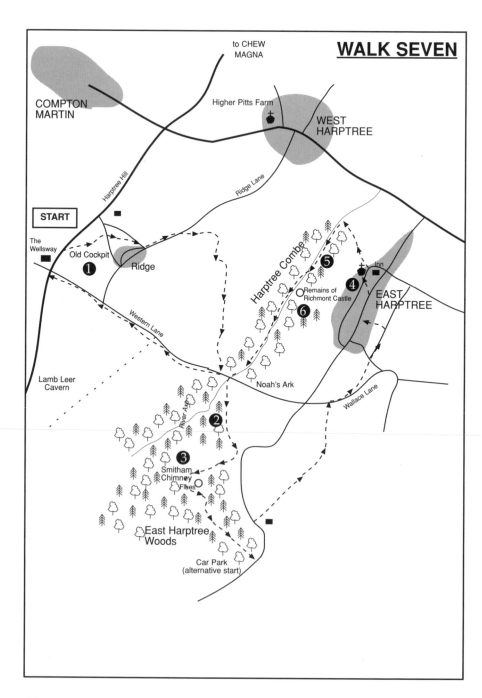

WALK SEVEN

to CHEW MAGNA

COMPTON MARTIN

Higher Pitts Farm

WEST HARPTREE

Harptree Hill

Ridge Lane

START

The Wellsway

Old Cockpit

Ridge ❶

Harptree Combe

❺

Inn

❹

EAST HARPTREE

Remains of Richmont Castle

❻

Western Lane

Lamb Leer Cavern

Noah's Ark

Wallace Lane

River Axe

❷

❸

Smitham Chimney

Flues

East Harptree Woods

Car Park (alternative start)

START at the welcoming and renovated Wellsway Inn above Compton Martin and West Harptree. This was one of four inns which served the old Bristol-Wells road where it crosses the Mendip plateau. This route had been abandoned as a main road by the time the Turnpike Commissioners took over in the mid eighteenth century. Park in the big car park below the pub in the top part where the landlord has kindly given permission for us to stop. It's a good place for refreshment. To reach the Wellsway, take the A368 from Blagdon to West Harptree and after going through Compton Martin, at a cross roads (where the inn is signposted) turn right up Harptree Hill marked to Cheddar which goes up over the Mendips. It is under a mile up the hill on the right.

Come out of the car park and turn left down the hill for 200 yards. Then go right over the stone slab stile on the marked path up a grassy track across the field. Already it feels like a good walk with pleasing views across Chew Valley Lake, a feeling of being high and out in the open along this northerly scarp. Head across to the left of the wooden house in the rectangular stone walled enclosure in the middle of the field – which is not what you might expect! It is in fact, an old cockpit **(1)**.

Having read Robin Athill's Old Mendip, *which mentions that one could see the site of a former cockpit above West Harptree – a stone walled rectangle of a certain size – I set out to find it. The ordnance survey map showed such a walled area in the middle of this field and I eventually tracked down farmer John Burge, who has lived here all his life; he confirmed that this was it. He remembers when the field was called 'cockpits'. It seems to have been the custom for cockpits to be sited outside a village away from prying eyes, although cockfighting as such was never actually illegal. So pause for a while and imagine the betting, baiting and fights that must have unfolded years ago in this beautiful spot.*

At the end of the enclosure, bear down the field to a cottage in the corner. Go over the stone slab stile and down the cottage drive to the lane. Respect the cottage owner's privacy and don't be too scared of the two rather noisy spaniels! Cross the lane and take the stile opposite. Go straight across the field, dropping down the bank to a stone stile on the far side. You are now in the hamlet of Ridge (once called Rudge). Turn left on the lane downhill, ignoring a farm track on the right. At a fork take the right-hand lane and continue downhill. After about 400 yards come to a stile on the left and opposite it a small unmade track/lane. Turn right down this lane, round a right bend (where it may be rather wet) and then round a more gentle left bend. After 150 yards go right over a marked stile in the hedge. Go up the field bearing slightly left. Take the wooden stile rails in the hedge up ahead and go over into a rough area. Go straight across to an opening in the hedge. In the next field follow the left-hand hedge and then bear right downhill to a stile by a gate onto a lane at an area called Noah's Ark.

Turn left and after 80 yards take the stile on the right by a gate. Go up the field to a stile in the top right corner. Go over and immediately left over another stile and up the field. You will pass a big depression in the field – a natural sinkhole in the limestone. Go over a stile at the top into the next field and straight ahead. Then over a stile by a gate and along a track. Turn right at the end and go up the metalled track towards woodland. Take the stile into the woods and then follow the path. Shortly you will see on the right remains of slag from the resmelting. Further up alongside the path you will see horizontal depressions on the right-hand side.**(2)**

These were horizontal flues built along the ground between the chimney and the furnace. The smoke from the furnaces which smelted the lead contained much lead vapour and this was precipitated on the sides of the flue on its way to the chimney. This lead deposit was then scraped off and sold.

Come up to Smitham Chimney **(3)** and the pond alongside.

Smitham was a word used in the re-smelting business and referred to the pieces of ore allowed through the wire bottom of the sieve. This impressive tapering chimney, very much like the mining chimneys of Cornwall, is made of limestone for the lower two thirds and the upper third is brick. It carried away the fumes when the crude mineral was resmelted. There have been two main stages of restoration – in the 1970s and in the early 1990s with the Mendip Society, the Mendip Area of Outstanding Natural Beauty Warden Service, the Countryside Commission and Forest Enterprise working together to ensure that the chimney remains as a

Smitham Chimney

'monument' to the hard work of the miners. It is the only remaining of four lead smelting chimneys on the Mendips. East Harptree was one of four lead reeves or lordships on Mendip which administered the mining rights. The mines were re-worked in the seventeenth and eighteenth centuries for short periods and again in the mid-nineteenth century, when there was an important revival in the Mendips based on re-smelting the extensive spoil-heaps left by the old miners. Many Cornish miners came in and worked them and did quite well for short periods until the end of the century. Much hard effort went into setting up the resmelting processes by the East Harptree Lead Works Co. Ltd established in 1867. The chimney, reservoir (the pond by the chimney), the buddles, flues and furnace were built but it was all closed down after ten years as output was insufficient. Once again, man had played a small part in shaping history and the world we see today.

Pass the chimney on your left and then go left up a path alongside the pond, keeping it on your left. Then follow the path away from the pond and on through Frances Plantation, an area of 197 acres planted in memory of Frances, Countess Waldegrave. Turn left on a broad stony track through East Harptree woods, with good views across the lake and valley. Pass a large public car parking area (*an alternative starting place, but be sure you leave no valuables in the car*). Turn left and follow the road gently downhill for 300 yards. Ignore two footpath signs on the right and take the third – over a stile into a field. Bear slightly left down the field to a marked gate. Head straight down the next field to another marked gate and then follow the left hand hedge down through two fields, leaving the last field by a gate in the bottom left corner, through the marked gate (which may now be a stile). Join a track and pass a Bristol Waterworks installation on the right – part of the line of works taking the pipeline to the Barrow Tanks near Bristol. Come to a house with impressive topiary yews by the gate. Turn right on Wallace Lane and follow it down to the dip.

There used to be a stone bridge taking the footpath over a water splash, but now both splash and bridge have been removed by the local authority. On the left are the ruins of an old cottage remembered as having honeysuckle over the doors and two skip beehives among the flowers on either side. 'Old Mrs Edwards, a noted laundress, used to stand white-aproned and white-haired, looking up over the sweep of Mendip before her, and so completing an unforgettable picture' – (From a history of the village by the Women's Institute).

Take the second footpath on the left, over the stile. Bear right across and down the field to a stile in the right-hand hedgeline. Cross the road and take the lane opposite – Water Lane. The land on the corner on the left is the site of the old village pound.

Go along this pretty village backwater with steep banks. Take the marked footpath on the left over an old stone slab stile and up the field with a hedge on the right.

This is Haydons Field. You may be able to make out odd bumps and humps. It is thought that this was the site of the early village which was subsequently moved further down the hill.The village is now a very pleasant and affluent community, with many of the old cottages and homes comfortably converted. Agriculture and mining for lead and calamine were once the mainstays of East Harptree: the whole village is honeycombed with old mine workings.

A stile brings you onto a lane. Turn right past a line of council houses on the left and go left up steps, over a stile and through a residential area. It is possible to cut off the corner by taking the stiled and waymarked footpath right across the field and come out by the pub. Or, come to the corner and simply turn right down to the church and popular pub, the Waldegrave Arms. Then cross over to continue the walk on the footpath at the side of the churchyard. However, it is worth visiting the church, though it may be locked – and for good reason! **(4)**

This pretty church has a light and airy feel. It has considerable Norman work and an interesting sixteenth-century monument in the porch to Sir John Newton with his twenty children dutifully kneeling in a row. I particularly like the Art Nouveau stained-glass window in the south wall of the nave commemorating the dead of World War II. The main figures are St Laurence, St George and St Agnes, and the small illustration under St George is of a mother and child waving goodbye to a man going off to join the army.

Sadly, one can no longer see the Roman coins which were one of the church's treasures for fifty years but were stolen in the early 1970s. They were part of the Harptree Hoard of nearly 1,500 coins found near Smitham Chimney in 1887 by a local labourer looking for fresh sources of water during the summer drought. The coins were discovered in a Roman pewter pot with some ingots of silver and a silver signet thumb ring. The find was examined by the British Museum and considered of great interest, not least because of the nine Roman emperors represented in the collection, all were Christians with the exception of one. This seems to testify to the existence of a Christian administration in this country some 700 years before the Norman Conquest. Fortunately, some of the rarer coins and the pewter pot were safely housed at the British Museum and did not end up in thieves' hands.

You will notice that the churchyard is higher than the fields around due to successive burials. The church path is made of old tombstone slabs laid upside down.

Take the footpath through the keyhole stile alongside the church and follow the path out through a similar stile. Cross the field, cross a stile and then walk along a broad grassy swathe between hedges. Go down towards the bottom, and then left over a stile into Harptree Combe **(5)** and follow the stream.

This is a beautiful area of mixed woodland where many wild flowers flourish, including the little known Herb Paris, once used as a cure-all for many different ills. Bluebell time and late spring is a good time to come here.

You reach an impressive aqueduct, part of Bristol Water's supply to Bristol.

This huge iron pipe was put up over 150 years ago and is still a remarkable construction. The whole line of works which took about four years to build using picks and shovels and manual labour takes water by gravity feed – no pumping – all the way from springs at Chewton Mendip to the Barrow reservoirs on the edge of Bristol – about 12 miles. The Mendip Hills are a vital water catchment area with 72 millions gallons pouring out each day.

Go to the right of the pipe. At the end of the walled enbankment on your left, part of the aqueduct, the path bears left and the stream carries straight on. Go a few yards on the path and then go up right on stone steps (if you reach a low stone wall on the left you have missed the steps). Follow this small path round and come above the stream. Up on top left of the mound is the site of ancient Richmont Castle **(6)** a notable stronghold for centuries.

The castle, set amid such beauty, must have seen much cruelty and many dramas. The original owner was the notorious Azeline de Percheval, so vicious that he was known as the Wolf, and his son, just as cruel, was called the Wolf Cub. Later it came into the ownership of the Gourney family (whose name lives on in the area in the form of Gurney). It probably had its uses in the Norman conquest of Somersetshire and was almost impregnable. In 1138 it was held for the Empress Matilda by Sir William de Harptree against Stephen, fresh from the siege of Bristol. He only managed to capture it through a ruse which lured the defenders out. The king, however, did not burn or in any way destroy the castle. It was not pulled down until Henry VIII's time.

Calamine mining went on spasmodically and in a small way around the site of the old castle until the mid nineteenth century.
Down on your right against the rocky side of the stream is the remains of a once much visited wishing well. Local people came here to drop a pin into the wishing well while they wished in silence three times, and drank some of the pure spring water out of the hand. It is now much silted up and the smooth circular stone basin around it invisible, but local history enthusiasts are keen to restore it.

Continue on the path following a leat and then pick up the stream and follow it up this magical green combe. When you come to a steep crossing path you can take the opportunity to go up the bank on the left and explore the site of the castle going left at the top along the edge. You may be able to make out the remains of some stonework but by and large there is nothing to see. But it is a beautiful spot shaded by magnificent beech trees. Some of the humps and bumps are the remains of the calamine workings.

To continue this walk, carry on up the combe, eventually reaching a stile at the end which brings you to a rough field. Cross the field to a stile on to the road at Noah's Ark – where you were earlier.

Turn right and follow the lane uphill, very steep at first, then more gentle and eventually flat with good views across the Chew Valley. Ignore any side turns. You are just on the edge of the scarp here with the typical windswept barren Mendip landscape on your left and the more wooded and habitated northerly sloping land on the right. After about three quarters of a mile reach a crossroads. Turn right to the Wellsway. It may well be open!

WALK 8

BEAUTY ON THE NORTHERN EDGE

Hinton Blewett – Litton – Cameley – Hinton Blewett

*Just on the edge of the official Area of Outstanding Natural
Beauty on Mendip, this walk offers views across the valleys
around Hinton Blewett and up to the Mendip high ridge.
It is a beautiful, gentle area of rolling meadows with attractive stone cottages and houses. In spring and summer it is a
good idea to take a wildflower book with you. The route
starts in the conservation area of Hinton Blewett, gently
descending to the reservoirs at pretty Litton, then along a
quiet lane and forest track before going through a nature
reserve meadow full of wild flowers. The main route goes
across fields to Cameley, with its appealing, unrestored
church and through meadows along the Cam back to the
start. The shorter route climbs up fields back to Hinton
Blewett. Before or after the walk it is worth driving to
Prospect Stile (Grid ref: 588 567) a few minutes to the west
of the village, from where there are stunning views over
Chew Valley and Blagdon Lakes.*

SPECIAL INTEREST: (see key on map)
1. Hinton Blewett church and village
2. Litton reservoirs
3. Old mill and button factory
4. Litton church and village
5. Nature reserve meadow
6. Cameley church

Distance: About 6.5 miles. Shorter route: 5.4 miles
Map: OS Explorer Map 4. Mendip Hills West. Reference: 595 569
Refreshments: Pubs at Hinton Blewett and at Litton
*Terrain: Walking is on quiet lanes and tracks and through fields, and you are likely
to encounter some muddy and wet areas. It is a mixture of flat, downhill and gentle*

WALK EIGHT

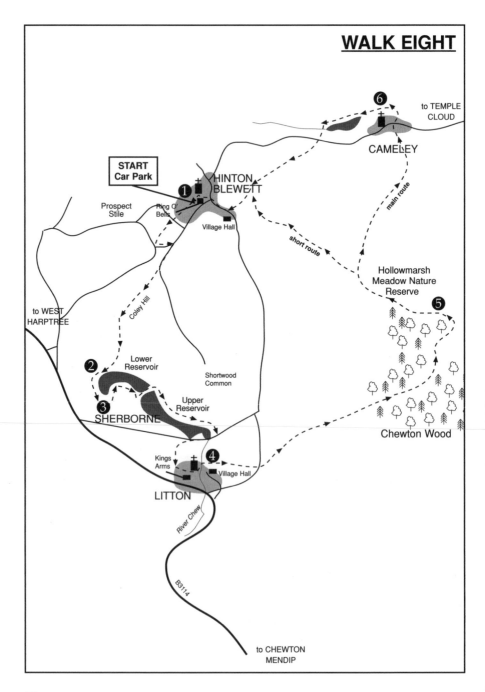

to TEMPLE
CLOUD

CAMELEY

6

**START
Car Park**

HINTON
BLEWETT

1

Prospect
Stile

Ring O
Bells

Village Hall

main route

short route

Hollowmarsh
Meadow Nature
Reserve

5

to WEST
HARPTREE

Coley Hill

Lower
Reservoir

2

Shortwood
Common

3

SHERBORNE

Upper
Reservoir

Chewton Wood

Kings
Arms

4

Village Hall

LITTON

River Chew

B3114

to CHEWTON
MENDIP

uphill walking, with one steepish ascent. It makes you feel that you've had a really good walk in beautiful surroundings.

START in Hinton Blewett which is a short distance south-south-east of Chew Valley Lake. It can be approached from the west from Temple Cloud, from the north from the A368 at Bishop Sutton or from the south from the B3114 between West Harptree and Litton. Park opposite the Ring O' Bells pub on the small village green, known as the Barbury.

Hinton Blewett (1) is picturesquely situated on high ground where there has been a settlement since Roman times. It was originally called Hantune – 'a settlement on high land' – and like many other villages the second name was added from the local landowning family, the Bluets who came on the scene in the reign of Edward II (1307-26). The small village green, church, manor, rectory, old farm and pub making up the centre of this village and because it is a conservation area the electricity power lines were all put underground a few years ago which is a real blessing. On the green where you park is a tree planted in February 1998 to celebrate the life of Diana, Princess of Wales. Sadly the oak which was originally planted did not take properly and at the time of writing there were plans to replace it with another tree, not necessarily an oak. Life seems to have carried on here fairly uneventfully for centuries with agriculture as the main industry. There is evidence that there may have been some mining.

Pass the pub keeping it on your right and turn right along to the church which has retained much of its old world charm and simplicity.

The Norman font is interesting as are the fifteenth-century bench ends which are arcaded and traceried. The tower was rebuilt early in the eighteenth century and the old tower must have been the one on which was displayed a quarter of the body of a supporter of the Monmouth Rebellion after being parboiled and dipped in pitch as a warning to others! There's an informative church history for those who want to find out more.

Continue along the road past the church and at a T-junction take the stile opposite. Shortly go over another stile and along the path. Over another stile and through the field following the left hedge and then cross left over a stile. Go right down the field heading to the right of a cottage and a stile brings you on to a lane. Turn left and then take the first right – Hook Lane. After a few minutes cross over a stile on the right. From here you have a view across to the Mendips and Smitham Chimney up in the trees.

Go diagonally left in the field and over a stile then continue in the same direction across the next field (keeping below the ridge) to the far hedge where you may think there isn't a stile, but closer inspection should find it, albeit fairly well concealed! The views get ever better and you can now see Eastwood Manor, the large grey mansion in the valley.

Cross the next field heading for the stile in the far left corner to the left of the telegraph pole. Cross and go straight ahead in the field and pick up a track following it down to the right. When it peters out continue on in the same direction down the field bearing left. Keep the hedge on the right and pass a group of ash trees on the right and a large oak on the left. Then take the stile ahead. In the next field follow the hedge down right. A stile brings you out at Litton Lower Reservoir. **(2)** Go straight ahead across the dam.

These two lakes – Litton Lower and Upper Reservoirs – were built in the mid-nineteenth century by Bristol Water when they piped the stream water to Bristol as part of their important line of works. The reservoirs ensured enough flow of water for the local millers even during drought. They are now used to raise trout for Chew and Blagdon lakes.

Go over the bridge which crosses the slip way and immediately past the cattle grid go left through the gate (which may be tied up with string) and follow the left hedge through the field to a double stile.

In the next field follow the left hedge along, ignore the path in the corner and then turn right following the edge of the field and then go left over a stile over a stream in the next corner.

(3). The stone building standing on its own by the stream on the right is something of a puzzle. Could it have been an old mill? The tithe map shows two mills at Sherborne a few yards apart – the lower mill was a grist mill. The feeling is that the building that remains here may have been the paper mill and local tradition has it that it was later used as a button mill. In the Litton census of 1851 Elihu Ticker was recorded as being a button dealer. Buttons were made from the horns of the cattle and water power was needed to turn the lathes while the horn was worked. Paper was an important industry in the Mendip area, with a number of mills harnessing the fast-flowing streams and using the clear water in the manufacturing process.

Having just crossed the stream, go immediately left along the small path by the water. Go over a stile, crossing the water to another stile.

This is a beautiful wild-flower area in spring, with bluebells, wild garlic, wood-ruff, meadow sweet, wood anemones, campion and brooklime (the very plain name for Veronica Beccabunga).

Keep following the path, which may be rather slippery and rough in parts, and find yourself close alongside the reservoir again. Eventually reach an area where the water is covered with nets – to keep the heron away from the young trout. Go up a flight of steps, then down steps and follow the path to a metal bridge across the run-off from the Upper Reservoir. Go across, up steps and ahead across the grassy dam. The reservoir on the right is still used as compensation so it may be very low at certain times of the year. Take the narrow footpath at the end which goes right between the house and the reservoir.

Along this path are a different selection of wild flowers including the beautiful-ly named 'Jack go to bed at noon' (because it closes at midday) and the tiny Moschatel – known as 'the town hall clock', which has five faces – one on each of the four sides and another on top so that aircraft going over can look down and tell the time! You may also see a variety of water birds, such as heron, coot, tufted duck, mallard and pochard.

Ignore two stiles on the left. Continue to the head of the lake and go left through a gap in the hedge and *straight* on to the lane – *there is no footpath so take care and don't let children or animals run ahead into the road.* Turn right and follow the lane over a bridge and along. Then turn left on a lane which passes a number of comfortable country homes. After a few minutes look for a short flight of stone steps on the left with a wrought iron gate. Go left up here and into the churchyard. **(4)**

St Mary's church has a fine tower rising in three stages and topped with battle-ments and pinnacles. Below the parapet are many carved corbels depicting heads of kings, bishops and others, as well as grotesque gargoyles. Inside, the four-teenth-century font is of particular note, carved with leaves and flowers and has an ancient pyramidal cover.

Go through the churchyard to the lane. Before continuing the circle, turn right on the lane, which immediately forks. Take the right fork for a few yards following the churchyard wall and look across to the hillside on the other side of the village where you may see remains of terraced farming in the form of strip lynchets.

These field systems date from the twelfth and thirteenth centuries. This was a period of rapid population growth. As more land was needed for crops, cultivation began to cover the sides of hills. The Black Death and dramatic decrease of population put paid to the need for the lynchets. The fields you see have never since been ploughed and so even seven centuries later it is possible to see signs of this medieval cultivation.

Retrace your steps to the fork, taking the downhill lane into the old part of Litton.

Litton, as it has been called since 1742 (originally it was Hlytton and underwent various changes over the centuries), has been predominantly an agricultural village situated around the stream, where three mills were once recorded. In the seventeenth century there was some speculative mining for coal, lead and other minerals but nothing significant was found. If it had, the development of Litton would have been quite different.

Come to the village hall on the left. If you want to visit the pub go on a yard or two to the well-known Kings Arms on the right, which has an extensive menu, many bars and a large garden on the other side.

The walk continues down the side of the village hall along the River Chew. Go over a stile and ahead in the field a few yards and then turn right up the field keeping a solitary ash tree on your left. Go over a stile at the top and straight across the next field to a waymarked stile by a gate. Cross the lane and take the small No Through lane opposite.

Follow it along for a good half mile until you come to the entrance to Chewton Wood. Go over the stile by the gate and follow the broad track straight on, ignoring a side track. There are a good selection of wild flowers to be seen along here. When I came in early summer, the lane was filled with wild roses on each side. When you get to a fork in the track take care to go left. Continue to the end of the track and cross a stile by a metal gate. Cross the lane and go more-or-less straight ahead over a stile by another gate into a field. Turn left along the hedge until you reach woodland on the left. Then immediately go left into the wood over a stile/bridge. Follow the path through the wood for a short distance and come into Hollow Marsh Meadow **(5)**.

This is a beautiful area of 4 acres of flower-rich unimproved natural grassland administered by the Somerset Wildlife Trust. It is at its height in late spring/early summer. Flowers include sneezewort, tawny and flea sedge, meadow thistle, heath spotted orchid, helleborines, fen bedstraw, bitter-vetch, saw-wort, marsh valerian and aspen.

Follow the path through the field and at the end go over a stile and bridge which crosses you from Somerset into Bath and North-East Somerset. Walk up this meadow which has a wonderful selection of wild flowers and butterflies and in spring is aglow with the yellow flowers of dyers green-weed.

This plant was found to produce a suitable yellow dye as a basis for making green and was thought valuable enough for the early settlers to take with them to New England when it was known under its old name of woad wax. It is now one of 'the naturalised aliens' of the eastern United States.

There are several stiles at the end of this field, so take care. Head for the far right-hand corner and take the stile ahead of you – not the stile on the right. In the next field go straight ahead for about 80 yards. You then have a choice: it is well worth going the longer route to Cameley if you can.

SHORTER ROUTE (OMITTING CAMELEY) – this is a reasonably steep climb at first. Continue ahead and follow the hedge on the right climbing up the field which is quite steep for a while. Look back and have a rest and you should glimpse the conical shape of the coal batch by Radstock in the distance. At the top of the field go right through an opening in the hedge, then left through a waymarked gate and immediately right through an opening into another field. Then go left following the hedge up the field. Cross a stile in the hedge at the end of the field and then go down the field with the hedge on your right. You are heading down to the small stream in the dip and then up the field on the other side, but to do this you have to bear over to the left so you can cross the stream. As you climb up the field on the other side bear back over to the right. Cross over a marked stile in the top right corner. Follow the hedge on the left straight ahead and as it bends left. You are now heading in the direction of Hinton Blewett church. Go over a stile and straight on in the next field; over another stile; straight on to a hedge corner. Stay in the field you are in with the hedge on your left. The right of way is now a little out of your way but please follow it. Go ahead, bearing diagonally right across towards the far right corner. Shortly before you reach the end of the field and the stream, turn 90 degrees left in the field and go along with the Cam stream on the right and joining up with *

MAIN ROUTE: Go through the gate opening ahead and then turn sharp right under an oak tree. Now just follow the right hand hedge through a number of fields. Pick up the waymark sign which directs you left in the field heading for the tower of Cameley church. Go over stile by a gate and out onto the lane in Cameley with a stable opposite.

Cameley was once a busy village, with brickworks and quarries. When these closed in the nineteenth century, and with the opening up of turnpikes, many people left the village, which had become little more than a hamlet. In effect, the village moved to the nearest turnpike, about $^3/_4$ mile east at Temple Cloud.

The circle continues by going left a few yards and then right over a stile into a field, but the reason for coming to Cameley is to visit the lovely little church **(6)** so go left along the lane a very short distance to the church entrance.

As you enter the churchyard, note the mounting block on the right just inside the wall. This is said to have been used by a former rector who used to ride over on horseback from the rectory near Hinton Blewitt and have his horse handy so he could get out to the hunting as fast as possible!

This simple wayside church is a real unspoiled gem, largely because restorers in the nineteenth century didn't get a chance to mess about with it and so the simple original furnishings, like the benches worn to a shine, have remained. It has great atmosphere. The nave walls lean outwards, the flagstone floors and burial slabs slope downwards. Light pours in through the clear windows onto the box pews dating from the seventeenth and eighteenth centuries. The tall one near the entrance was probably the churchwarden's pew with a high back to protect him from draughts. There was more seating up in the two galleries – the one on the south side of the nave was built in 1819 'for the free use of the inhabitants'. The wall paintings of which only fragments remain are one of the treasures of this small church.

St James's was once the centre of a thriving village of Cameley, but in the nineteenth century the population moved about three quarters of a mile east to Temple Cloud and a new church was built, leading to the neglect of St James'. In the last War because the roof was dangerous the church was closed. Later the nave was re-roofed and then a group of Friends led by Kenneth Gallop decided to seriously care for their little church. It is now 'a redundant church' looked after by the Churches Conservation Trust, but it is still a treasured part of the community.

A quick alternative now if the ground is wet underfoot is to continue on the lane past the church for about $^1/_3$ of a mile to the waymarked Limestone Link style on the left (then see below). Or to continue on footpaths, go back and over the stile just mentioned, before the stable. Go down the field following the left fence. Cross the stile in the wire fence near the bottom of the field on the left. Ignore the footpath down on the right. Go across the field bearing right towards the rather overgrown edge of the Cam stream. Cross a stile and continue on following the stream. Then cross the stream on a bridge and turn left with the stream on your left. Go past the fishing lakes, crossing a stile, and keep on along the stream to a double stile, which brings you into another field. Go straight on and shortly turn left over the stream. Head across the field with the hedge on the left to a waymarked stile by a gate. Go right on the lane and then almost immediately left over a stile picking up the Limestone Link marker. Climb diagonally right up the field to a stile. Once over, bear left up the field crossing to the top corner of the field woodland on the right. You may hear peacocks along here from the garden of the former Rectory, now called Cameley House.

Continue on in the same direction through fields. The Cam stream is flowing along over on the right. Two fields before the road, ignore a stile on the right. Just continue ahead in the field with Cam stream on the right *

*Both routes are now back together. Look for a stone slab stile in the far hedge to the left of a wide, often muddy, opening. Cross in to the next field heading for the stone slab stile in the far right corner and come out on the edge of Hinton Blewett.

Opposite is the former primary school, which is now the village hall, but happily it is used each morning as a Montessori nursery school and so is still alive with the sounds of children's voices.

Turn right up the lane back to the Barbary in Hinton Blewett where you parked.

GREEN AND UNDULATING

Dinder – Worminster – Croscombe – Dinder

Parts of this walk are reminiscent of the Cotswolds, with farms nestling in the folds of rounded hills. The walk, beautiful at all times of year, would be particularly reward- ing in spring, with the many different wild flowers to be seen in meadows, along the lanes and in the woods. There are stunning views down the valley to Wells and across the countryside. It takes in two very attractive Mendip villages with evidence of the former industry and prosperity of the area. It cuts through farmland, meadows of wild flowers and an Open Access area where farming is done without the use of chemicals.

SPECIAL INTEREST: (See key on map)
1. Dinder village, church and manor
2. Disused railway
3. Open Access area
4. Friar's Oven
5. Croscombe and Croscombe church.

Distance: 6.4 miles
Map: OS Explorer Map 4. Mendip Hills West. Reference: 575 445.
Refreshments: Pub in Croscombe (about three quarters of way round).
Terrain: Walking is along quiet lanes and footpaths, across fields and through woods. There is a balance of uphill, flat and downhill walking. Go well shod, as it can be muddy in parts.

START in the village of Dinder, about 2 miles south-west of Wells. Head out on the Shepton Mallet road – the Wells bypass – and look for a left turn to Dinder. Find somewhere safe to park by the beautiful old church.

This attractive village (1) nestles in a valley – the name Dinder means 'in a deep valley between high hills'. It was once an agricultural village with a thriving cottage clothing industry in the eighteenth century with its own leather mill. An

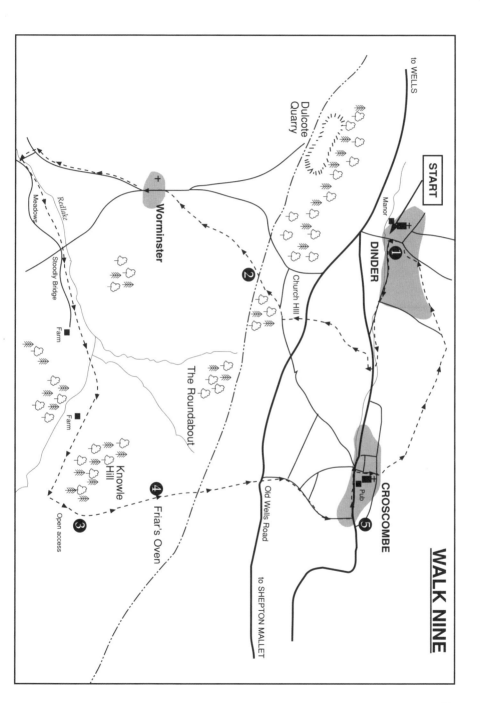

WALK NINE

START

to WELLS

Dulcote
Quarry

DINDER

Manor

1

Worminster

2

Church Hill

Meadows

Redlake

Stoodly Bridge

Farm

The Roundabout

Farm

Knowle
Hill

3

Open access

4 Friar's Oven

Old Wells Road

Pub

5

CROSCOMBE

to SHEPTON MALLET

81

attractive house is on the corner, opposite the church – seventeenth century Wisteria House (aptly named). It also has a decorative shell porch. Pilgrims en route from Winchester to Glastonbury often stopped in Dinder, washing their feet at the well in the orchard before spending the night at an old cottage rest-house nearby. Dedicated to St Michael, the small ancient church, formerly a Norman chapel, is well worth a visit. The lychgate and resting house for coffins are notable, as is the ancient twisted yew tree (one book suggested it was over 1,200 years old!) on the south side of the church. There's a nice piece of history concerning the church and the squire in Victorian times. When Squire Somerville used to line up his estate staff to pay them on Fridays he always asked if each man had been to church on the previous Sunday. If the answer was 'yes' the worker was given an extra half crown and the term 'half crown Christians' grew up.

You can get a good view of the manor – Dinder House – if you go round the other side of the church through the churchyard.

For long the home of the Somervilles, Dinder House is now the offices of Ecco shoes – quite appropriate that the village again has connections with leather. The last squire was Sir James Somerville who died at Dinder House in 1949 and was an Admiral of the Fleet.

To start the walk proper, come out of the churchyard, turn right and go right round the corner. Opposite the entrance to Dinder House turn left along the village street passing a line of pretty sixteenth century gabled cottages made from stone from Doulting quarry.

They face onto a leat formed from diverting the Doulting water (otherwise known as the Sheppey) which flows through the village, through Dinder House park, over cascades and under a bridge. One of the cottages was a former pub and still carries the sign of 'the Dragon on the Wheel' – the crest of the squires of Dinder, the Somervilles.

Just before the main road go left over a stone stile and through the field with the stream on the right. Cross a stile in the corner and follow the path between stream and sewage works. Turn right along the sewage works lane to the main road. Turn right and in 50 yards cross this rather busy road with care to take the marked footpath up the field.
Go up following the left hedge. Cross a stile into Cliff Wood and then go right on the path which climbs up through the woods to a stile in the top corner.

Follow the hedge on your left, enjoying good views down the valley. Continue on through two more fields and go over a stile in the top left corner onto a lane. Take the stile on the other side of the lane a few yards to the left. Go ahead along the right hedge and just before the end of the field cross a stone stile right and go through a small patch of trees on to a lane. Turn right. After 150 yards take the marked footpath left descending into the valley. Go over a stile into a field and ahead, bearing slightly right, keeping the island of trees and scrubland on your right and then head across a short distance of field to the fence line. Go right along it a few yards to a stile. This crosses the old disused railway line **(2)**.

It is part of the East Somerset Railway, which ran from Witham to Shepton Mallet and opened in 1858. Four years later the line was extended to Wells and there were plans to take it through Croscombe, but landowners objected strongly to this. The Great Western Railway took over the line a few years later and it closed in 1964. Part of this line near Wells has been used as the bed of the new bypass, sadly filling much of this beautiful valley with traffic noise.

Go over and take the stile into a field and climb up bearing diagonally right heading for the top fence and a wooden post. There's a good view from here across to Dulcote Quarry.

The quarry is where Foster Yeoman began his quarrying business in 1923. He did so with a labour force of 100 former soldiers. Today Foster Yeoman operates two of the largest stone quarries in Europe, one of which is Tor Works near East Cranmore on the Mendips. Some quarrying still goes on at Dulcote but not at peak level. Expansion of the quarry was stopped some years ago by local pressure because it was felt it would cut away the view of Dulcote Hill from Wells.

Go left through the gate by the post and through the field following the hedge on your right. You can still enjoy good views back to Wells and the soaring tower of St Cuthbert's (the largest parish church in Somerset) and now also a lovely panorama across rolling countryside and across to the plateau of Worminster Down, ahead on the right. Up on the left is a round hill, the Roundabout, topped by a reservoir. At the end of the field carry straight on along a track and descend the hill gently. Go right over a stile and head down the field bearing diagonally left towards the farm barns on the other side of a sunken lane. Go over a stile and down steps and turn left on the lane through the hamlet of Worminster.

There is a legend possibly connected with Worminster about Bishop Jocelyn of Wells saving the hamlet from a marauding serpent or dragon by killing it. Could the serpent have given rise to the name 'Worm' in Wormister? There was another worm found in the wall of the chancel of Dinder church. It had a head at each end and is believed to date from the earlier chapel on the site. It now rests above the rector's stall – was this the Worm of Worminster?

You pass an ancient wayside cross on the right. Stay on the lane for about three quarters of a mile, passing Wootton Vineyard (although it may well not still be running on a full commercial scale) and other attractive country homes. Ignore a lane on the right, cross a stream and then turn left on a No Through lane which is metalled. It becomes rougher and 60 yards on go over a stile straight ahead into a field. This is one of a series of lovely flower meadows which you now walk through keeping the hedge on your left. Go over a stile onto a crossing track (Mill Lane). Turn left and follow the stream on your left to Stoodly Bridge. Cross the lane and go straight ahead on a farm lane through a gate.

Just before Red House Farm take the stile on the left. Go down the field to a gate in the bottom right corner. Go through and then ahead a few yards with the stream on your left and go left through another gate. Walk down the length of the field making for a stile and footbridge close to the far left hand corner ignoring a footbridge on the left en route. Cross the stream and on the other side follow the fence on the right up the field. Go over a stile on the right and then head across the field bearing left towards a gate. Just before the gate, turn right along a grassy track between hedges which brings you to the farm. (If it is very muddy and impassable along here, an alternative is to stay in the field and walk parallel to the track keeping it on your left. This brings you back on to the track by the farm.) Follow the farm lane along between hedges, climbing the hill and after about a third of a mile, at a junction, you will see a marked footpath on the left and information about the Open Access area you are about to enter (3).

This is 14 hectares of undulating limestone grassland farmed without the use of chemicals. A number of different plants flourish in this environment including cowslips, salad burnett and common milkwort.

Go straight ahead up the field at the top of which there are three gates. Take the small wooden hunting gate at the side of the middle gate and climb diagonally left up the field to the top hedge and along, turning right through another hunting gate. Go slightly left in the field, which has the feel of parkland, passing a modern house over on the right. Go through a waymarked gateway and straight down the next field. Up on the right is a rocky outcrop of Carboniferous limestone known as the Friar's Oven **(4)**. Go through a gate and over the stone stile behind it and bear right across the field to the raised wooded embankment of the disused railway line (the same line you crossed earlier). Go along below the embankment keeping it on your right and then go through the railway bridge and bear left across the next field towards a farm. Leave the field by a very short track and come on to a track known as Dungeon Lane. Follow Dungeon Lane to Dungeon Farm.

Dungeon Farm in the mid-nineteenth-century is thought to have been a hiding place for smugglers' booty – mainly brandy and silk brought in from the Severn estuary. The silk was hidden in sacks of potatoes and brandy.

Pass a large chicken shed on the right, at the end of which turn right and head for a wooden kissing gate on the far side of an area of tree planting. Go through and bear right up the field to a gate on the top which brings you onto the Old Wells Road. Cross over and take the lane opposite, heading down towards Croscombe. Fork right onto another lane and follow this all the way down the hill to the main road in Croscombe **(5)** by an attractive old stone bridge, Prosperity Bridge, built for the former chemical works.

The bridge was renamed Folly Bridge when the chemical works of J.E. Woods failed. The works was set up in the mid-nineteenth century to process chemicals reclaimed from the processing of iron ore mined locally. (The two bungalows near the bridge are on the site of the old works.) There were high hopes that this new venture would replace the declining woollen industry but it soon failed leaving huge debts. Across the road is the old Manor, an early Tudor building. On the left of the house is a 'Drink and Thank' plaque on the wall where a stand pipe was installed by Croscombe Water Company. Croscombe owes its former prosperity to the woollen industry and as this died out other small industries were attempted such as mineral mining, chemical manufacture and silk.

Turn left passing Griffin Mill.

This old mill is on the site of the earliest mill along Doulting Water. The stream is divided into two in order to provide enough water for another mill.

Take the slip road with the stream on your right, passing the elegant Old Rectory. Rejoin the main road. Cross with care. Turn left along the road, crossing Rock Street (note the appropriate name of the cottage at the bottom of the street!). You soon come to the welcoming Bull Terrier (formerly called the Rose and Crown), one of Somerset's oldest pubs, with an ale licence dating back to 1612, and outside the pub is Croscombe Cross.

This was saved and retained in its original position due to action by villagers. Authorities tried to move it to make more room on the then narrow and winding road for the first traction engines. But villagers picketed it to prevent them from moving it.

From the pub turn right up Church Street to the church.

St Mary's church is very attractive. Inside there is a feast of Jacobean wood carving including the fine rood screen, pulpit and box pews. At the south west end is the two storey treasury, once the meeting place of the seven Guilds of Croscombe. Later it was also the parish lock-up and the parish armoury. The church dates mainly from the fifteenth and sixteenth centuries and instead of the usual Somerset tower it has a spire. The present one replaced an earlier spire, hit by lightning in 1936. It is in complete harmony with the rest of the church because the owners of the quarry from which the first was made reopened it so that suitable stone could be obtained.

Come out of the church back on to Church Street with the small old tythe barn opposite. Turn right up the hill and then left into Fayreway. Go over the stile on the right and bear left across the field, clipping the edge of the school playing field and continue up to the top corner, over a stile. Continue straight ahead along the edge of the hill through fields heading towards Dinder. If you look across the valley you should be able to see the ridging of the old strip lynchets used for cultivation. When you reach a small lane turn left and after 200 yards, at the corner, take a stile on the right and head down the field bearing left. Go through a gate and down the next field and through another gate. Bear left across a small field and out through a small gate onto a lane.

This intriguing wooden 'concertina' gate (see illustration) is one of two on the estate at Dinder made by a local man, Percy Hull about fifty years ago. It won him first prize in the Bath and Wells Show. It was not in a very good state of repair when I used it.

Go left down the road and then along to the church and the start.

PAST THE LOST VILLAGE

Nettlebridge – Ashwick Grove – Stoke Bottom – Edford Meadows – Harridge Wood – Nettlebridge

Nettlebridge village sits on the ancient Roman road known as the Fosse Way (now by-passed by the main road). It is in more recent history, in the aspirations of John Billingsley, an agricultural pioneer who helped shape the Mendips as we know them, that this walk has its origins. The route follows the path by the stream through beautiful woodland, which runs from the site of his home at Ashwick Grove to the ruins of Stoke House and papermill at what was once the village of Fernhill. Enjoy a tantalising stretch of what remains of the Somerset and Dorset Canal and at the right time of year catch a glimpse of the past in the shape of traditional hay meadows at Edford, as well as wild daffodils along the way.

SPECIAL INTEREST: (see key on map)
1. Nettlebridge Valley
2. Lime Kiln Lane
3. Ashwick Grove and John Billingsley
4. The lost village of Fernhill and Stoke House
5. Dorset and Somerset Canal
6. Edford Meadows

Distance: 5.5 miles. Shorter Route: 3.25 miles
Map: OS Explorer 5 Mendip Hills East. Reference: 648 484.
Refreshments: Nettlebridge Inn, and the Duke of Cumberland at Edford
Terrain: *Walking is on quiet lanes and footpaths across fields and through woods. As usual wear suitable footwear for comfort and protection from the wet and mud.*

START at Nettlebridge in the large car park behind the Nettlebridge Inn. We were told that the management is willing for walkers to park in the car park and it is a good place for refreshment before or after. Nettlebridge is between Radstock and Shepton Mallet on the busy A367, just south of Stratton-on-the-

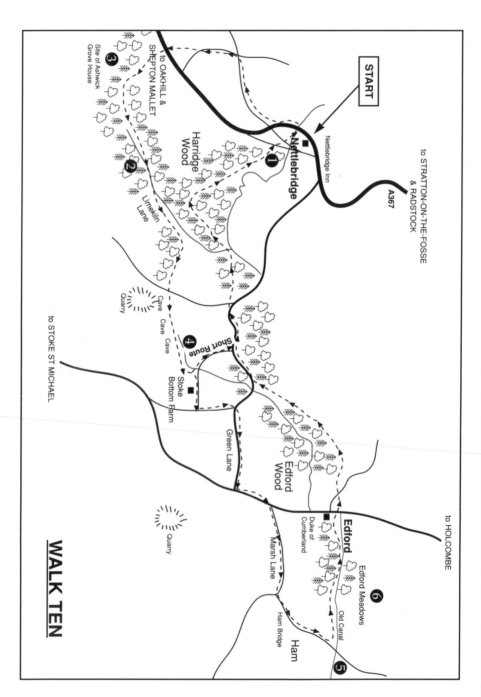

WALK TEN

Fosse. The inn itself is on the A367 as the road descends into the Nettlebridge Valley **(1)**.
WALK: leave the Nettlebridge Inn car park and go left.

The Nettlebridge Valley was an early centre of coal-mining. Situated not far from Shepton Mallet with its reputation for manufacturing 'fine knot hose,' Nettlebridge also had a role in that industry. Just how big is hard to say. A so-called 'stocking factory' at Nettlebridge may have been a warehouse where finished products were collected. An extensive 'stocking manufactury' was advertised for sale at Ashwick in 1796. And as late as 1872, William Urch of Nettlebridge is described as a 'hosiery manufacturer'.

Ignore the footpath sign on the right and start up the slope. Shortly, across the road you will see what looks like a concrete drive with a sign on the wall indicating 'Bag End'. Cross the busy road with care and continue up the 'drive' which soon becomes a country lane. Continue on, passing a farm and houses until you reach a junction. Turn left in the sign-posted direction of Bath. A hundred yards or so on, where the road bends left, cross over the stone stile on your right into a field. Continue in the direction you have been walking which will take you diagonally across the field to the far corner and the A367. You will see the footpath sign ahead. Cross over the road and over another stone stile into a field. The footpath sign indicates you should bear left across the field but if it is cultivated it may be better to walk around the edge. If you do this, continue down the field with hedge and bungalows on your right to the corner. Turn left and continue with fence on your right until you meet the stone stile. You will be paralleling the path you will eventually join. Cross over the stone stile into Home Wood and follow the path down hill: there's a lovely decaying, moss-covered stone wall for some of the way. Soon you reach the valley bottom and what is now Limekiln Lane **(2)**. Turn left.

*Limekiln Lane links the site of Ashwick Grove **(3)**, the home of one John Billingsley, which was demolished in the 1950s with Stoke Bottom and what was once Fernhill, a village which has long since disappeared. The lane forms part of what was probably one of the carriageways to Ashwick Grove, but now, down in the valley amidst the trees, with the gently flowing stream and perhaps the scent of wild garlic, it is difficult to imagine what things could have been like 200 years ago. John Billingsley (1747-1811) was a man of substance. 'He drained Sedgemoor! He enclosed Mendip! He wrote the agricultural* Survey *of* Somerset!' *it was said in a tribute shortly after his death. The* Survey, *written*

Leaving Limekiln Wood

in 1794 for the recently formed Board of Agriculture, at a time when the country needed to increase food production after the outbreak of war with France, was indeed a major achievement for it gave us the Mendips as we know them today. Robin Athill, in his book Old Mendip, *says, 'The familiar landscape of the main Mendip Plateau with its wide straight roads, grass bound and grey walled, its scattered farmhouses, each with a sheltering windbreak of trees, is a landscape which Billingsley did much to create.' A founder member of the Bath and West Society he also introduced the double-furrow plough to Somerset. He had many other interests, often linked to progress, including the new turnpike roads and canals. Towards the end of the century, he was the owner of Oakhill Brewery, involved in the Kennet and Avon Canal and the Dorset and Somerset , which, as planned, would have served Mendip collieries within a mile of Ashgrove.*

Continue on with the stream on your right and note how the flow picks up as it is boosted by more and more water from the hills. Note too the increasing evidence of man's engineering, what have been described as 'lion cages,' and eventually a leat as the path approaches the ruins of a gamekeeper's cottage. Beware – this and other ruins on the way are potentially dangerous: resist the temptation to go exploring and stay on the path.

The water engineering which you have passed was almost certainly the work of Billingsley or, later, the local authority as they attempted to make the most of the water which flowed from the Mendip Hills. The leat was probably Billingsley's attempt to channel water to the water meadows ahead. He would have, no doubt, walked this way. He once owned the mill at Fernhill, now Stoke Bottom, but appears to have sold it via an advert in the Bristol Journal *of July 31, 1784. Today, depending on the season, you can enjoy the beautiful moss covered rocks and walls, snowdrops, anemones, violets, bluebells and wild garlic.*

Home Wood, Limekiln Wood and the two parts of Harridge Wood (which you will pass through later) are owned by the Somerset Wildlife Trust. All three woodlands lie on the site of former ancient woodland. Harridge Wood and Limekiln Wood were felled and replanted with conifers and poplars by the Forestry Commission in the 1950s and 1960s. The Trust has recently purchased these three woodlands and plans to restore them to broadleaved woodland over the coming years.

Go over the stile beside the gate ahead and into what were the water meadows. Continue around the edge of Limekiln Wood on your right. When you reach the road, cross over and go through the gate opposite. There's an old ruined cottage above you and, out of sight, a disused quarry and, as marked on the map, Fairy Cave. But none of this is accessible, so continue on with a hedge on left – where it survives – note the way in which it has been cut and layered in the traditional manner. Soon, you reach a bubbling outflow of water which flows immediately under a lovely arched bridge. This is St Dunstan's Well, still pouring forth. Go through the gate, along the track until you reach the road. It is clearly walked. Stay on the track, close gates and generally respect the property. Take care, there are ruins ahead and at one point the water plunges down a steep hole, so keep children close by.

The ruins include those of a papermill and as you go further along, those of Stoke House which stood amid the bustling community of Fernhill (4). There is not much to see now but history records that at one time or another Fernhill boasted a logwood mill and paper mill in a hamlet of about forty houses which included a Georgian mansion. The population numbered about 200. The mansion, Stoke House, which was unconnected with the local industry, except by location, took full advantage of the water and was on a grand scale. It is said to have had splendid staircases, an Adam fireplace, stables, outbuildings, lawns and pleasure gardens in 5 acres of land with 10 acres of woodland and pasture. According to one description 'water was led through the garden, over falls, under arches and between walls of stone, cut with care and set in cement, that must have cost a little fortune in their day.' From 1778 until the mid-nineteenth century, the mansion was the home of the Chichester family, but by the late 1920s it had been abandoned and was crumbling. The paper mill and surrounding cottages had been abandoned earlier, certainly by 1841.

Go through the gate and onto the road. It is worth taking a few steps left and looking over the wall for another view of what is left of Stoke House.

(If you wish now to take a shorter route – Route B – continue up to the T junction: the main walk passes this junction on the way back, see below)

To continue the main walk, about turn and head towards Stoke Bottom Farm. At the end of a line of farm buildings, just before the farmhouse turn left up a wide farm track which is also a bridleway. Continue on to the road, turn left and then right along a straight stretch of road. At a junction, with quarry workings over to your right, turn left and take next road to your right which is known as Marsh Lane. Turn left at the junction, signposted Coleford and cross over the pretty stone Ham Bridge and continue up the hill a little. It is worth noting the lovely old Ham Mill on your left. Shortly go left on the marked footpath and continue keeping the hedge on your left. As you enter the woods you are walking along the towpath alongside the bed of the Dorset and Somerset Canal **(5)**.

The Dorset and Somerset Canal was one of a number of abortive attempts to construct an inland waterway to link the Bristol Channel and the English Channel. This stretch was part of a planned 11-mile branch canal from Frome to Nettlebridge. One report said it was costed at a little over £30,000, but that something like twice this amount was spent and the branch line was still a couple of miles short. The project went no further. John Billingsley was one of the backers. He is said to have subscribed £3,500.

Soon, up on your right , you will see the fields know as Edford Meadows **(6)** and owned by the Somerset Wildlife Trust. At certain times of the year they may look like any other fields, but they are very special.

The have been recognised as a Site of Special Scientific Interest. Most of the land has been managed as traditional hay meadows at least since the Second World War. After haymaking the fields are given over to grazing by cattle. There has been virtually no use of agrichemicals. As a result the meadows are a good example of unimproved grassland and, in summer, provide an all-too-rare glimpse of what the traditional hay meadow looked like. Access is along the foot-path to prevent damage to the hay crop.

Stay on the path and continue on. The path cuts across the corner of one of the meadows and goes on into the wood. It is clearly marked and you are proceeding, over a number of stiles, with the River Mells down on your left, until you come to the road, with the Duke of Cumberland public house with its garden and stream down to your left. Cross over and head for the bridge ahead.

This was the first bridge going over the Dorset and Somerset Canal – a packhorse bridge – carrying the old road from the coalpits on Stratton Common down to Edford – for a brief moment old and new ways of transport crossed.

Drop down off the bridge and contour round the top of the field, keeping the wood on your left. The footpath may not be clearly marked at first but you soon pick up a track which passes over a stream and through a gate, keeping the wood close by on your left and open fields on your right. Following the edge of the wood, you eventually arrive at a road. At the road, turn right with Harridge Wood on the right.

Shortly you will reach the T-junction referred to earlier in Route B. It is signed 'Stoke Bottom Farm'. Those who have taken the short cut, turn left.

Those on the main walk continue on until you reach a signpost. It indicates Nettlebridge to the right, but you go over the wooden stile alongside a gate ahead and slightly to the right. There is a choice of path here, but keep to the lower level with the wood on your left and go over a stile into the wood (it is still Harridge Wood) with the stream tight on your left. Shortly there's a lovely old bridge. Continue on up to a clearing and take the clear track to your right. Follow this track all the way back to Nettlebridge.
Eventually you exit from the woods via a gap alongside a wooden gate onto the loop road that serves Nettlebridge. Go down the road into the valley bottom and just before the telephone box turn left into the village itself. Shortly, there's a footpath, right, which cuts across a small field and back up to the A367 and the Nettlebridge Inn.

IN THE FOOTSTEPS OF THE MINERS

Coleford – Vobster coke ovens – Vobster – Coleford

East Mendip's industrial life at present is centred around the quarry industry. However coal-mining was the lifeblood of the area for centuries. This quiet walk is through beautiful countryside in the midst of which can still be seen the remnants of the mining industry rapidly crumbling as nature takes over. It is a route which gives a good feel of the unique attraction and history of this area where man has toiled over centuries to extract the wealth lying under the soil.

SPECIAL INTEREST: (See key on map)
1. Wesleyan chapel
2. Remains of old Dorset and Somerset Canal
3. Vobster Breach colliery and coke ovens
4. Vobster
5. Newbury works
6. Old Waddell fan
7. Hucky Duck
8. Mells Stream and mill
9. Cottages in Coleford

Distance: 5.3 miles
Map: Explorer 5 Mendip Hills East OS. Reference: 686 486
Refreshments: Pub in Coleford and Vobster
Terrain: It's easy walking mainly on footpaths and tracks which, particularly along by the river, can get muddy and slippery. There are no long, hard uphill climbs or sharp descents.

START in the village of Coleford, south of Highbury and north of Leigh upon Mendip. Park at the King's Head down in the old part of the village by the river where the landlord has given walkers permission to leave their cars. In return it might be a good idea to have a drink at the pub.

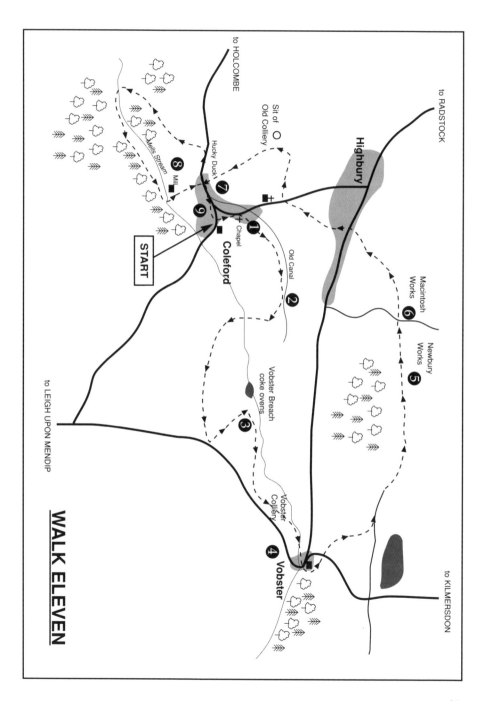

WALK ELEVEN

START

to HOLCOMBE

to RADSTOCK

to LEIGH UPON MENDIP

to KILMERSDON

Coleford

Highbury

Vobster

Sit of
Old Colliery

Chapel

Hucky Duck

Mill

Mells Stream

Old Canal

Vobster Breach
coke ovens

Vobster
Colliery

Macintosh
Works

Newbury
Works

① ② ③ ④ ⑤ ⑥ ⑦ ⑧ ⑨

95

The King's Head was built in 1742 and seriously damaged by fire nearly a century later in 1830 It was so well patronised that the owner, John James arranged for rapid refurbishment and it reopened the same year. Rumour has it that a ghost lurks upstairs and unlatches the clubroom door! Coleford means the ford over which charcoal was carried or where coal was found.

Turn right out of the car park and immediately turn right again on a narrow cobbled path up the hill (not the path that goes along the back of the pub). Come up to the road and turn right, continuing uphill past cottages in Coleford – many of them built of local brown ironstone and pass the converted Sunday School which also became the Day School in the 1830s. You soon reach the impressive Wesleyan Methodist Chapel on the right **(1)**.

Methodism was very strong in Coleford fuelled by frequent visits from John Wesley himself. He took a keen interest in the building of the first Methodist chapel dated 1746 – one of the first in the country – which was thatched. It was pulled down in 1860 as it wasn't large enough and the present grand three-storey building put up. The village population had swelled by this time and mining in the area was doing well. It is still used as a chapel today.

Just past the chapel squeeze right through the wall into a field. Go straight down with a line of trees on the right and reach a big wide 'ditch' – the remains of the bed of the old Dorset and Somerset Canal **(2)** (see Mells walk for more details). Follow it along and go through the iron barrier ahead and then another barrier and come onto a raised embankment – part of the old towpath. The old canal is now on your left and then it seems to peter out. Go through a barrier, straight across the field towards woodland. Go over another barrier by the wood.

On the left is what looks like more signs of the old canal and in fact it is believed that this was the entrance to the canal tunnel which was planned through the hill at this stage. (You reach the end of the tunnel later in the walk.) It seems uncertain whether the tunnel was ever completed.

Follow the path along the wood edge and then over a wooden barrier and turn right downhill to a stile into a field. Go down and cross the lively Mells Stream. Head for the far left corner of the next field. It's a good point to look back at Coleford village and the very different skylines of old and new houses. Go over a stile and follow the right hedge (passing a gate in the corner) through the next two fields. Ignore stiles on the right. Go through into the third field and head straight across to a stile. Go over the stile and left and then left again onto a track which leads to the Miners Pond fishing area. You are heading for the end of the track, but if the second gate is closed use the stile/fence on the left. After the third gate you come into the site of the former Vobster Breach Colliery (3). There is no public access to the site so stay on the footpath.

There is much evidence underneath the ivy and undergrowth of former industry when this was a busy mine supplying coking coal for the Westbury Iron Works. In 1860 a new 860-foot shaft was sunk to replace an earlier one and a steam winding engine fitted. It was, in fact, the last pit in Somerset to use water powered pumps. From Vobster Breach a narrow gauge tramway took the coke to the Vobster incline (you are going this way) where it was hauled up the hill and loaded onto the railway. This colliery was part of the southern area of the Somerset coalfield, probably the earliest to be worked and was at its busiest throughout the nineteenth century. Very few mines survived beyond 1920. The Somerset coalfield was roughly a triangle from a northern point at Pensford southwards for about 11 miles to a base along the Nettlebridge valley from Gurney Slade east nearly to Mells.

Go ahead into the centre of the open area and turn right on the green swathe (this is the footpath, not the next green track by the old coal batch). You pass between a line of rare, but crumbling coke ovens, walking along what used to be the old tramway sidings.

These old ovens are the showpiece of this site. They are long, not beehive shaped as elsewhere, and are the only ones of their type in the Somerset coalfield, dating from the mid nineteenth century. There were a double row of twelve on the left and a single row of twelve on the right. They are now listed and many local enthusiasts are keen to see them preserved and saved from further crumbling.

At the end follow the marked path left round the end of the ovens with the old colliery batch (spoil heap) up ahead. Turn right over a stile and bridge. You head across the field and in the distance should glimpse Mells Park.

This is a mansion rebuilt by Sir Edwin Lutyens after a fire in 1917 on the site of a Georgian mansion built by the Horner family of Mells in the eighteenth century.

Go through a gate and ahead in the next field, following the line of the old

Dennis Sleigh

Coke ovens at Vobster

tramway (you may just be able to make out a raised bank). Over on the left in the hedgeline is the leat which was part of the extensive system which took water along to the waterwheel to pump out the pits. Go over a stile where on the left is a large wooded coal batch (spoil heap) and remains of buildings both here and a little further on the right. This is the site of Vobster Colliery which linked up with Vobster Breach.

It closed in 1874, the same year as Vobster Breach and had three shafts – two for winding and one for pumping. Winding was by steam, but pumping was water powered. Fire damp was a great danger in this coalfield and there were a number of serious explosions. There are records of one in 1865 which was strong enough to 'blast people out of the mine'.

Cross the next field bearing left to a stile. Then turn left, cross a ditch, a small field and then Mells Stream. Two more stiles bring you out onto the road in the hamlet of Vobster **(4)** – which I found a surprising community, so well restored and manicured that it no longer seems to have any feel of having once been a mining area. Turn right and come to pretty Vobster Inn – a good place for refreshment.

To continue the walk go through the garden and car park and up the wooden steps behind.

On the right is the former incline plane up which the trucks of coke were hauled to the railway at the Mells Road junction.

Go steeply up the hill and take time to look back across Vobster.

Although the unseasoned eye (like mine) can see no trace on the slope of the field, all along the valley on the other side of the hamlet there were once at least fifty bell pits. Outcrops of coal on the surface here were worked very early on by individuals and their families, who dug out shallow bell-shaped pits to extract coal and then moved a few feet away and dug another. This continued until the advent of mining technology and the sinking of deeper pits. The first documentary evidence of these pits is 1305 but they could go back to Roman times.

Cross right over a stile at the top. Go left down the field to a stile onto a road. Cross with care and turn left down the road for a short distance to a wooden kissing gate by a main gate. Go up this path lined with alders, through another kissing gate and in front of old Vobster church, now discreetly converted into a private home.

This is an early Victorian building (1848) by the diocesan architect Benjamin Ferry and modelled on the chapel of Merton College, Oxford with lofty hammer-beam roof.

Go through a third kissing gate and ahead in the field up the old church path. If you look across to your right you should see the raised green embankment of the old canal. Follow the path up to cottages – the line of the old canal and later the Newbury railway which served Newbury Colliery was through what is now their back gardens. Turn left on the lane. Disused Vobster quarry (now full of very deep water) is up on the right. When you reach the No Through Road sign go ahead on the track on the left which is the line of the old canal and then railway. Cross the stile on the left and continue in the same direction along the old line through fields all the way to Newbury Works **(3)** (ignoring side paths) where stone blocks are now manufactured.

This is the former important Newbury Colliery, which produced a good-quality coal for nearly 130 years until it closed in 1927. It was a very deep mine, with a shaft of nearly 2,000 feet. The coal was very suitable for coke production and the coke went to Westbury Iron Works which owned the colliery. There used to be large coke ovens at the colliery for the conversion of the coal. The coke ovens were pulled down in 1950 when the site became a stone works.

Go straight ahead in the works where it is important that you stick to the footpath as this is a working industrial area. Keep to the left of the large building. Then turn left halfway along the building. Then turn right with the embankment up on your left. Follow the path up.

Over on the right you can see the tall old stone Cornish engine house which contained the beam engine to pump water out of the mine. It came to the pit secondhand from Cornwall and is now a listed building.

At the top of the path, go right, then left and reach the access road to the works. This formed part of the old steam-driven narrow gauge tramway up to Mackintosh Works. Follow it along to the end with a miners cottage over on the left and it's here that the other end of the Dorset and Somerset Canal tunnel was sited.

Cross a lane and take the path ahead. Go up the track, which can sometimes be very muddy and dirty as a result of use by farm vehicles. As it bends to the right look up on the left and you will see a crumbling arch.

This is all that remains of the building that housed a Waddell Fan (6) at the former Mackintosh Colliery. This is the last remaining such fan in the area. It was a rotating drum with discs which blew fresh air down one side into the mine and drew the foul air out the other side. Nearby is the capped remains of the shaft into the works sunk in 1867 in order to increase output from Newbury Works and to comply with new safety legislation which said that pits had to have second shafts for escape purposes. This was linked to Newbury underground. Mackintosh closed in 1919 after it was flooded and the Newbury works continued for a further seven years. Its closure marked the end of a long period of mining in this area.

Continue on the track and follow it round left down the hill, ignoring the stile on the right. Take the right-hand fork following a fence on your right and gradually go down to a stream. Cross, go over a stile and then through a stone keyhole stile, up a drive and up to a road in the top of Coleford – the area known as Highbury. I like the quote on the Temperance Hall across the road – 'Woe unto him that giveth his neighbour drink and maketh him drunken *also'*. Go left and then turn right down Carey's Mead and as the road bends right take the path straight ahead. You are heading in the direction of Coleford church. Follow the path down to the road and turn left passing Coleford Schoolroom on the left – note the arched recess in the wall, one of several in the village where the old water stand pipes were sited. Cross and take the track opposite the old schoolroom, or you may wish to visit Coleford church beforehand.

The church, dated 1831, is in the Gothic in style and has an unusually spacious interior with an aisleless nave. It has a utilitarian and stark feel – probably very much what the miners liked in their place of worship.

Cross the stile and go ahead down the field towards the trees. Go through the gap in the trees and then up into the field and continue on through into the next field and on again following the hedge on the right. Turn left along the top of the field at the next line of hedgerow trees. Ahead of you in the wood on the right (off the public right of way) is the site of an old coalpit, but there is nothing to see except a few hummocks.

This was Coal Barton pit which, with Newbury, was the most important pit in the area. In the mid nineteenth century there is a record of 130 people working here Coal Barton saw the second worst pit disaster in Somerset in 1869, when nine miners were killed from an explosion of firedamp caused by ventilation problems.

The official footpath bears left back down across the field (which you have just come up) towards a kink in the hedgeline. Then follow the lefthand hedge bearing down and go left at the end. Go ahead through the next field. Coleford church is ahead on he left on the hill. At the end of the field, don't start to climb up, but instead turn right and go along to a stile. Now follow the path all the way along the valley until you come to a famous local land-mark, the Hucky Duck aqueduct **(7)**. (This was the access path to the coalpit.)

Hucky Duck is local dialect for 'aqueduct' and was the largest of the works com-pleted on the ill-fated Dorset and Somerset Canal. It was topped with a fancy balustrade but this has now been removed and probably used in large houses in the area. It was designed to take the canal over the Coleford valley. The few miles of canal from the Hucky Duck to Edford was the section finished and may have been filled with water and even carried a few stone barges – but who knows? It is a local, much photographed landmark.

Go under the Hucky Ducky and out onto the road in Coleford. Turn right up Springers Hill. *(However, if for any reason you need to cut the walk short turn left and follow the road down to where you parked.)* By the derestriction sign turn left on the marked path alongside a bungalow – the site of a former village pub, the Greyhound Inn which closed in 1912. Follow the wall straight down. Go over a stile and along the field with hedge on right following the line of the old canal. Go over a stile into a pretty area of woodland where you may at the right time be able to see early purple orchids.

You can see what looks like a pond. This was probably the one and only turning basin on the canal

Continue on, over another stile, and turn left down the field, ignoring the marked path which goes ahead. Come to Mells Stream **(8)** and follow it along right through pretty woodland and come shortly to a bridge. Cross the stream and then turn left with the stream on your left, ignoring the footpath signs to the right. Follow the stream through woodland – a mass of garlic and wood anemones in spring and where you can see some fine examples of polypods (ferns) growing on the trees across the water – and through fields with stream on left, across a field, over a stile and into woodland. Eventually you reach a field, going a little away from the stream. At the end of the field take the left of two gates and bear left across the field back down to the stream.
You reach the old Packsaddle Bridge (the sides of packsaddle bridges were kept low so that goods were not easily knocked off the backs of the animals). Cross the bridge. (If you come at daffodil time you might like to make a small detour before you cross the stream – continue on the same side for a short distance and you come to a wooded area which is a mass of wild daffodils.) After crossing the bridge you pass an old mill.

This is one of two mills in the village. There is evidence of the Knights Templar having a corn mill here in the thirteenth century and there was probably a mill on the site much earlier.

Come up to the road in Coleford and turn right. At one time or another all the cottages **(9)** you pass along the road were probably little shops. On the left was the Rose and Crown, another of the village locals. Go steeply down the hill. Over on the right is a large house which is known as the former doctor's house, and the last house in the terrace on the left before you reach the Kings Head was the isolation hospital.

BEAUTY MASKS AN INDUSTRIAL PAST

Mells – Conduit Bridge – Barrow Hill – Buckland Dinham – Great Elm – Mells Stream – Mells

A good alternative is to start at Buckland Dinham

This is a 'plumb' walk in the Eastern Mendips in more ways than one. It is reputed to be the home of Little Jack Horner, and is a beautiful area of greystone villages, high open land and rugged mossy and ferny combes alive with flowers, bird and butterflies. But, crumbling away under all the beauty there is much evidence of an amazing industrial past where hundreds of people toiled for many long hours. This is a walk of contrasts, with good views across valleys and open farmland as well as a long stretch along a deep rocky river valley.

SPECIAL INTEREST: (see key on map)
1. Mells village – many different buildings of architectural and historic note including the fine church. What was Jack Horner's 'plum'?
2. Remains of the abandoned Dorset and Somerset Canal.
3. Evidence of a successful lever lock on the old canal
4. An old coal mine
5. Buckland Dinham village, church and lock-up.
6. The crumbling and ivy-covered remains of what was one of Britain's most thriving empires – Fussells, iron tool makers for nearly a century.

Distance: 6 miles
Map: Explorer 5 Mendip Hills East OS. Reference: 727 492
Refreshments: Pub in Mells and in Buckland Dinham
Terrain: This interesting walk has a few uphill and downhill sections, but no espe-cially arduous stretches. Walking is on footpaths across fields and along quiet roads and lanes, as well as along a riverside path.
Special note: You can equally well do this circle from Buckland Dinham (parking

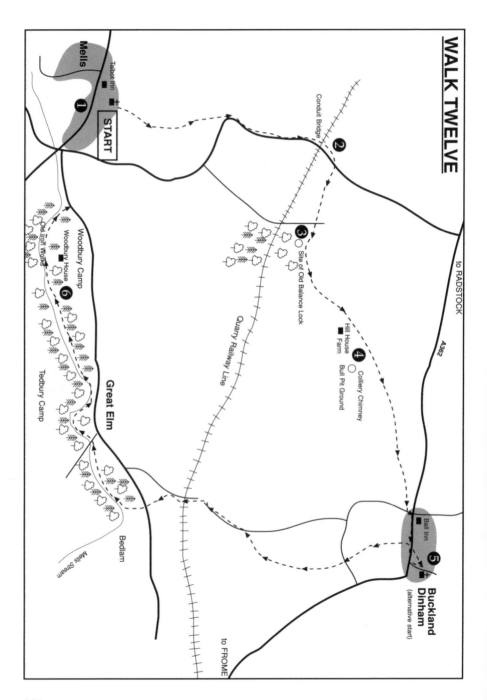

WALK TWELVE

Mells

Talbot Inn

1 START

Conduit Bridge

2

to RADSTOCK

A362

3 Site of Old Balance Lock

Colliery Chimney
Hill House
Farm
4
Bull Pit Ground

Quarry Railway Line

Old Iron Works
Woodbury House
Woodbury Camp
6

Great Elm

Tedbury Camp

Bedlam

Mells Stream

Bell Inn
5
Buckland Dinham
(alternative start)

to FROME

104

near the church) and have the interest of the Fussells works and Mells in the middle. Turn to page 108 and start from the church.

START in the village of Mells **(1)**. Find somewhere safe to park near the Talbot Inn. Turn down the side of the inn into a picturesque short street (New Street).

This street was designed in about 1470 by Abbot Selwood of Glastonbury Abbey. It was meant to be the start of a town plan in the shape of a cross, but only New Street was ever completed. Of particular note is the boys' school on the right, built in 1840, with a plaque commemorating the Golden Jubilee of Queen Victoria.

Go through to the fine fifteenth-century church.

The church's most obvious outstanding feature is the tower – a fine example of a Somerset Perpendicular. The faceless clock on the tower strikes the hours and the quarters and every three hours beginning at midnight, it plays one of four tunes. There's a warm welcome. In a small area near the main door is everything necessary to make coffee is left for visitors to help themselves!
The church contains much fine work by Burne Jones, Gill, Lutyens and William Nicholson who were friends of the Horner family, the lords of the manor of Mells. In the Horner Chapel is a memorable statue of Edward Horner on horseback. It was the first venture into sculpture of the distinguished painter of horses, Sir Alfred Munnings. Edward was the last direct male heir to the estate.
There are some fine monuments in the churchyard, including one to the First World War poet Siegfried Sassoon, who died in 1967. He asked to be buried here beside Ronald Knox, the distinguished Roman Catholic priest and scholar who lived in Mells Manor while translating the Bible.
The lawns of the churchyard spread out towards fields and up to the wall of the Elizabethan Manor of Mells.
Mells is forever linked with the old nursery rhyme of little Jack Horner. There are many versions, but one is that Jack was a scullion in the Abbey Kitchen of Glastonbury at a time when Mells was owned by the Abbot. He, in an effort to save his property at the time of the dissolution of the monasteries, sent the deeds to a place of security, hidden in a pie, entrusting it to Jack Horner. Being hungry, the boy promptly opened the pie and discovered 'the plum' – the deeds, and thus became the owner. It's a good story, but untrue and unfair to the Horner family as Mells was bought from Henry VIII by Thomas Horner and the legal deeds proving this were preserved.

The main industries for Mells revolved around the fast flowing Mells Stream. There is evidence of a corn mill in the Domesday Book, then fulling mills for the thriving cloth industry in the Middle Ages (at that time Mells even had its own woad plantation for dyeing) and later the river was harnessed to power machinery for the world-renowned edge-tool industry. Today quarrying is the only remaining significant industry.

Leave the churchyard round the back up the eye-catching avenue of clipped yews designed by Sir Edwin Lutyens and out through the very unusual stile, dated 1857 – one of only three which survive, invented by Thomas Lyne of Malmesbury.

Go slightly right up the field and through a gate to the next field. There's a fine view behind of the church, Mells Manor and village behind. Go straight across the field to a gap in the hedge and then in the next field head for the far left corner (go round the edge if the field is planted with crops). A stone stile brings you to Conduit Lane where in season you may find the beautiful Common Star of Bethlehem along the verges. Go straight ahead and before long come to Conduit Bridge over the railway line. A few yards after the bridge you may be able to make out signs of the old Dorset and Somerset Canal **(2)**.

Plans for the canal began at the end of the eighteenth century during a time of canal mania. The main canal was intended to link the English and Bristol channels (from Poole to Bristol) to avoid the long, dangerous passage around Land's End) and to connect with the Kennet and Avon Canal. The plan was initially to build this 11 mile branch from Frome along the Nettlebridge valley to serve the local collieries and link up with the Somerset Coal Canal. Royal Assent was given on March 24, 1796. The building started but only nine miles was completed and the main canal never even started. It fell foul not only of the expense and preoccupation with the war with France, but also money became scarce due to a slump in the woollen industry, the mainstay of the area.

Continue for 150 yards up the lane and take the marked footpath on the right, going through a narrow band of trees to a field, and continue along the top of the field with the fence on your left. You are walking parallel with the old canal which was down in the valley to your right. Go over a stile, cross the track and over the stile opposite. It's then ahead in the field bearing slightly right to a gap in the fence. Then go ahead a few yards to a fence ahead and a grassy track running left/right. Down in the trees ahead on the right in a deep depression, is all that remains of the revolutionary lock **(3)**. It is not on the public right of way, however.

This Balance or Lever Lock (or caisson lock) was designed by the ironmaster from Mells, James Fussell. It is overgrown now, and much of the masonry has been removed; water has long since left the canal bed so it requires imagination to envisage the scene on September 6, 1800 when to great acclaim the first trial of this great new lock took place. It was designed to get boats up and down the gradient on Barrow Hill. Barges were floated into large watertight boxes or 'caissons' made of wood or iron which fitted snugly the channels of the canal and the chambers of the lock. The caissons were simultaneously raised and lowered like balance scales by means of racks and pinions connected to a beam going across the partition wall which divided the lock in two. The chamber was to be 88ft high, 20ft wide maximum in the middle, and 88ft long. Boats were taken up and down a fall of 20ft and it was acclaimed as being cheaper and quicker than any other lock so far. It was decided to build five similar lifts on the canal between Mells and Frome, but money was fast running out and there was a fear of invasion from France, so in 1803 work on the canal ceased 'until more auspicious times arrived'. By the time money was more available, railways were in vogue and much of the canal became railway bed. Nine miles of the canal were completed, but there are hardly any traces now of the canal, locks bridges, tunnels or aqueducts. This is one of only a very few places where you can get any idea of what was achieved (see walk for more traces of the canal and aqueduct). Some sections of the canal still had water in them as late as 1840. The canal disappears at this point to appear further on, but about a mile east alongside the railway line below Barrow Hills are the barely visible remains of four pits from a second of Fussell's balanced locks.

To continue the walk, return to where you joined the grassy track. Follow the track with the fence on the right for 80 yards and go left up into a field. Turn right along the field edge and along to a stile. Then follow the hedge to the left in the next field and leave by a gate at the end. Go along a track to Hill House Farm and continue on. As you go along the track, you can look across on your right to an old colliery chimney above a disused mine shaft and slag heap (or dirt-batch) almost hidden by trees.

This was the mine (4) of the Buckland Coal Syndicate which dug a hole 96-foot deep but the venture failed because the mine was continually flooded.
There has been mining in North Somerset for centuries, but it was not until the seventeenth century that mining activity really stepped up in the area. Conditions particularly for children were appalling. Wages of boys were 1s 6d (7 pence) for a week for working barefoot and often naked, lugging a heavy 'putt' or sled loaded with several hundredweights of coal through the candle-lit darkness

underground. There were many hazards including collapsed workings, poor ventilation, gas explosions and fatalities from fire-damp (methane). By the beginning of the nineteenth century about 4,000 people worked the coalfield, but some of the older, small pits began to close. All pits closed by 1973.

On the right of the mine is an area marked on the ordnance survey map as Bull-Pit ground, which could either mark an old bull baiting ring or simply be a reference to a useless – or in old English 'bull' – unproductive coal digging.

The sport of bull-baiting was not made illegal until 1835. Robin Atthill in his book, Old Mendip, *tells of older generations who knew the field you are looking at as Blood Field.*

Follow the track all the way to a lane. Turn left and come into Buckland Dinham **(5)**. Turn right and pass the Bell Inn, a welcoming place for refreshment. Carry on along the pavement alongside the main road passing a number of interesting old cottages and houses.

The village owed its prosperity to the manufacture of cloth in the fifteenth century. Teasles were grown locally to dress the cloth. The village was also renowned for its ancient weekly market to which pedlars flocked , and the annual three day Michaelmas Fair. Shrove Tuesday was apparently the occasion for a cock throwing contest. A bird was put in an earthenware vessel with his head and tail free, and contestants had a go at throwing the pot. Whoever broke it and freed the bird, claimed the poor unfortunate as the prize!

You come to a flight of stone steps on the left. Before continuing this circular walk you may like to make a very short detour and see the old village lockup and church. To do this continue along the main road. Turn left at the end and go up to the church of St Michael's with its attractive restored lychgate. Just before the church on the corner on the left is a small building with a tiny barred porthole – this was the guard house used as a lock-up for the disorderly.

The church was built in the twelfth century by Oliver de Dinan, descended from the family which came to Britain from Dinan with William I. Parts of Oliver's church that remain today include the main south entrance and the north doors and the two windows in either wall of the nave. The twelfth century font and the fifteenth-century roof of the porch are outstanding features of the church. The tower is Late Perpendicular, about 1480. You may be fortunate enough to hear the set of eight bells being rung – it is a sound that was silent for thirty-nine years until the end of December 1994 after a complete re-hanging and overhaul of the bells, frame and fittings.

Then come back to the bottom of the flight of steps. Cross the road at this point and take the track between cottages. Pass garages and a playing field and go through a kissing gate, then over a stile and straight ahead on a well used path. Cross a well-worn stile and down the field offering good views over the valley.

The Macmillan Way signs along this part of the walk refer to a long distance path of 290 miles from Boston in Lincolnshire to Abbotsbury in Dorset. It was set up in 1995 to raise money for Macmillan Cancer Relief through sponsorship of those tackling the walk. For details contact: Peter Titchmarsh, St Mary's Barn, Pillerton Priors, Warwicks, CV35 OPG.

Cross a stile on the left and bear left down the field to yet another stile onto a lane. Cross and go up and over the stile opposite and straight through the field to a double stile and bridge. You need to go diagonally right across the field to the second gate on the far right side, but if the field is planted you may need to continue straight on and then turn right across the field. Go through the gate; cross the track and take the fence/stile into the field opposite. Follow the right hand hedge up the field and go over a stile on to a lane. Go left on the lane and continue on until you go under a rail bridge. Take the first gate on the left. Go up into the field and across to the far side to a fence/stile onto the main road. Cross with care and go right for a few yards. Turn left down a lane to a very pretty area at Mells Stream. Ignore the footpath going straight ahead. Turn right over the stream and then right through a kissing gate onto a path which runs alongside the fast-flowing river so much the life blood of Mells. Immediately on the right you will see the remains of an old mill in the middle of the stream. In Spring the valley is a mass of snowdrops and later with violets and monkshood. Go under the railway bridge and on, passing in a few minutes a beautiful converted mill house. Continue to follow the stream and come out onto the road by the bridge at Great Elm.
Turn right on the lane, cross the bridge and continue up the hill. At a right hand bend go left on the marked path over a stone stile and follow this down to the Mells Stream. Continue through rugged Wadbury Valley. Steep cliffs on the other side climb up to an important Iron Age promontory camp of

Tedbury and the whole valley is a green and secretive confusion of under-growth hiding remains of the former industry and workers' homes.
You go through a manicured lawn area with houses up on the right. Continue on, following the footpath which hugs the stream (don't go up the drive). Before long you come to old walls on your left and the first signs of what was the main iron works. There are glimpses through the crumbling walls of what was once one of the biggest industrial sites of its kind in Europe **(6)**. If you carry on to the end of the long high wall you may be able to turn left down into the site which was the main Lower Works. Originally there were large entrance gates here and the building with the beam sticking out was the office. Take care looking round as there are many deep pits and unsafe crumbling masonry. If access to the site is now restricted due to safety reasons, please respect any warning or no entry signs.

From the mid-eighteenth century until the end of the nineteenth century work-ers toiled under 'the iron rule' of the Fussells' family to make the name of Fussells of Mells known throughout the Empire.
A main reason why in 1744 the Fussells took over the derelict iron works of James Naylor and began their empire was the powerful supply of limestone water which was especially suited to hardening the edge-tools. There was a local source of coal for the furnaces, but it is not obvious where the main supply of iron came from.
Water drove the tip hammers, bellow and other machines. There was a complex series of buildings, tunnels, leats, thirty-five waterwheels, a dam, covered canals, forges, a rope walk for ropemaking and even a bakery for the workers! Most of the records were lost so we do not have the complete picture, but thanks to the work of a team of local historians and architects who spent seven years excavating the site in the 1970s, we know a lot more.
The site was immense. At its height, there were between 400 and 500 people working at these two Mells sites alone.
The Fussell's business expanded quickly until there were six separate sites in the area producing edge-tools such as hay knives, scythes, billhooks spades, shovels. In order to produce a very sharp edge to the iron tools it was necessary for the worker to lie flat on a board very close to the grindstone – a dangerous and dif-ficult job – which probably gave rise to the expression 'putting your nose to the grindstone' ?
By the start of the 1800s Fussells was exporting to Europe and America. During the Napoleonic Wars James Fussell was prompted patriotically to offer the gov-ernment 1,000 pikes and then later 2,000 each week.
The demise of English agriculture in the 1870s had a great affect on this empire

and Fussells seemed not to adapt quickly to new techniques and fell behind rivals. In the 1880s the business was taken over by Isaac Nash from Worcestershire and by 1895 all production had ended. Now the noise of the ironworks has been replaced by birdsong. Where workers toiled in the tunnels, horseshoe bats have sought sanctuary. There is a chance that the site may be purchased and preserved for archaeological purposes and/or wildlife.

As you leave the site, continuing on the main path, you pass on the right the crumbling remains of the Spadetree works, where there was also a ropewalk.

It was at this works that wooden handles and ropes were produced.

The open area you come to marks the site of the Upper Works of Fussells.

All six sites were probably connected and there may have been transport by means of flat bottom boats between them.

Come out onto the road. Turn left. Note the smooth rounded tops of some of the walls here. These are grinding stones taken from the Fussells' site. Go along to a junction where over on the left is a memorial to Mark Horner – a Community Water Tap and Shelter.

This was designed by Sir Edwin Lutyens. On Mark's death in 1908, Lady Horner paid for water from the manor reservoir to be piped into the village.

Go ahead on the Coleford Road, passing the little post office on the right Over on the left is a large seventeenth-century building, the Clothier's Mansion, and at the next junction there is more of Lutyens' work – a war memorial where the names of those who died, regardless of rank or social standing, are listed in alphabetical order. Continue on, passing a fine fifteenth-century tythe barn in the yard on the left, now used as a village hall. Continue on to the Talbot
(If you started at Buckland Dinham, the walk continues up the street at the side of the Talbot – New Street [turn to the start of walking instructions]).

REFERENCE MATERIAL

Old Mendip. Robin Athill. David & Charles.
Mendip - A New Study. Robin Athill. David & Charles.
The Heart of Mendip. Francis Knight. Chatford House Press.
The Sea Board of Mendip. Francis Knight. Alis Press.
The Mines of Mendip. J.W.Gough. David & Charles.
Colliers Way. Peter Collier. Ex Libris Press.
The Mendips. Coysh, Mason and Waite. Robert Hale Ltd.
The Dorset & Somerset Canal. Kenneth Clew. David and Charles.
The Mendip Hills - a threatened landscape. Shirley Tolson. Victor Gollancz.
The Origins of Somerset. Michael Costen. Manchester University Press.
Some Buildings of Mendip. R.D.Reid. The Mendip Society.
The Somerset Landscape. Michael Havinden. Hodder & Stoughton.
The Buildings of England - North Somerset and Bristol. Nikolaus Pevsner.
Penguin Books.
Shipham - a local history. Michael Matthias.
Trinkums-Trinkums. Kettlewell (memoirs of East Harptree).
History of Wookey Hole (written by Mrs Atthill for WI Competition 1953,
entitled The Story of our Village).
Villages in Avon. Avon Fed WI. Countryside Books.